A SUMMER TO REMEMBER

For Annabel

England v Australia 1981

A SUMMER TO REMEMBER

PATRICK EAGAR
with commentary by Alan Ross

COLLINS
St James's Place, London, 1981

First Published in 1981
by William Collins Sons & Co Ltd.
London . Glasgow . Sydney . Auckland
Toronto . Johannesburg

Photographs © Patrick Eagar 1981
Text © Alan Ross 1981

Designed by Ronald Clark
Photoset in Century Schoolbook by
MS Filmsetting Ltd, Frome, Somerset and
Printed by William Collins Sons & Co Ltd, Glasgow

All the photographs have been taken by
Patrick Eagar with the exception of:
page 48 top, by Eric Beecher; page 127,
by William Eagar; page 128 top right, by
Jan Traylen

ISBN 0 00 216388 8

CONTENTS

INTRODUCTION

It is remarked, often enough, by novelists that characters sometimes take hold of a plot, adapting it to their own ends. The Test Matches of 1981 proved such an instance, when a handful of cricketers achieved, as if they were fictional characters, a life of their own quite independent of the parts assigned to them.

A Test series that began on June 18 had proceeded predictably by July 21 to a point where the narrative line appeared to have been decided. When play began on July 21 England, 124 runs ahead of Australia with only one second innings wicket in hand, were on the verge of defeat. Australia, as much through appalling English catching as anything else, had won the First Test by four wickets. The Second Test, at Lord's, had been drawn; rain had taken a goodly chunk out of it and Botham, England's captain, had made nought in each innings.

Brearley led England in the Third Test at Headingley, but even his mystical persuasiveness had failed to galvanize England's batting. Facing an Australian total of 401 for 9 declared England were shot out for 174, Botham making 50. Following on they were reduced, by the early afternoon, to 133 for 7 wickets. The match, if not the series, seemed virtually to be over.

It was at this point that the characters, for the first time, showed reluctance to be imprisoned in their destiny. Dilley, after scoring 11 runs in 7 innings in the West Indies, hit the besieging Australian attack all over the field to score 56. With Botham he put on 119, 8 runs short of England's eighth wicket record against Australia, set up by Hendren and Larwood at Brisbane in 1928/29. Botham, in one of the most savage Test innings of modern times, went on to score 149 not out.

On the last morning Australia, soon taking England's final wicket, were left to score 130 to win. When they had reached 55 for 1 shortly before lunch the routine nature of their task looked to be confirmed.

Willis now changed ends and within a few balls transformed the match. Pounding in and drawing undreamed-of resources, it seemed, from some compelling interior vision he took 8 wickets for 43 in 15.1 overs, Australia losing their last 9 wickets for 55 runs and the match by 18 runs.

If there were illusions now that the sickly pattern of England's batting failure had been broken they were quickly dispelled. At

Edgbaston England were bowled out for 189 and, trailing by 100 on the first innings, set Australia only 151 to win on a good wicket and in perfect weather. Australia looked in no real trouble, Border and Yallop making 58 together for the fourth wicket. Emburey then disposed of these two and Botham polished off the match by taking 5 wickets in 6 overs for 1 run. Australia, with a golden afternoon suddenly idle on their hands, were beaten by 29 runs.

At Old Trafford England again batted dismally, losing 9 wickets for 175 on the first day, Botham making 0. Australia collapsed in their turn, and then England, with a first innings lead of 101, looked to have thrown their advantage away by losing half their wickets for 104. At half-past two, however, on a sultry Saturday afternoon Botham emerged from the gloom of the pavilion to play a second historic innings. During the morning England had taken 34 overs to score 34 runs against Alderman and Lillee, losing four wickets in the process. In the personal equivalent of fourteen overs Botham now scored 118 runs, the last 113 of these coming in 70 balls, mostly off the new ball. Jessop's great hundred at the Oval against Australia in 1902 had taken 75 balls.

Australia, left the hopeless task of making 506 to win, got to within 103 of them. Yallop and Border, the former almost effusively, the latter nursing a broken finger, stoically, made hundreds and at two different stages of the innings – when Yallop and Kent were together, and later Border and Lillee – Australia had glimpses of the unattainable.

With the series won and the Ashes retained, the Sixth Test match at the Oval should have been a relaxing affair. But it, too, developed into an absorbing, fluctuating encounter, England holding out for a draw after being in dire danger of defeat for most of the last afternoon. This, then, was the strange pattern of events, totally unpredictable at the outset and dramatically disturbed in match after match. At the end of a summer that began with weeks of cloud and rain and finished in the bluest of Augusts, the whole thing, to English eyes, had an air of fabled magic to it. To Australians listening and watching across a continent stretching from the Swan River to the waters of Sydney Harbour, it must often have been an unbelievable nightmare.

FIRST TEST

TRENT BRIDGE (18–23 June)

On paper there appeared little between the two sides. England, battered by the West Indian fast bowlers throughout a disturbed and chastening winter, had a chance to redeem themselves on their home grounds and in conditions familiar to them. The Australians, their preparations upset by atrocious weather, had suffered further from injuries and the hospitalisation of Lillee with bronchial pneumonia. England could look forward to a respite from real pace, the Australians, bolstered by undoubted superiority at their last encounter, to continuing their improvement. In the event England batted and fielded in the most disappointing fashion. Australia, though batting little better, emerged as the more resourceful and determined side. Moreover, Lillee, bowling well within himself and at no more than fast medium, proved that the great bowlers can succeed through the deployment of their skills as much as through sheer pace. The wild card, in this match as in all the others, was Alderman, a medium paced bowler from Perth, who in his first Test match took 9 wickets for 130. Alderman, in conditions not far removed from those at Perth, bowled 24 successive overs at the start of the match to take 4 for 68. Well-built, heavy footed, and with a perpetual grimace that looked from a distance like a grin, Alderman kept the ball well up and swung it disconcertingly. Only Gatting, carrying the fight in his usual pugnacious manner, and Dilley, flailing around at No. 9, made batting seem other than a struggle for survival. Lillee, conserving his energies and employed in short spells, used variations of pace and the width of the crease to confound each batsman in turn.

England bowled no less well until a succession of dropped catches – five in all, most of them depressingly simple – demoralized them. Australia recovered from 89 for 6 to 179, only six short of England's total.

England fared even worse in their second innings, Alderman bowling throughout to take 5 for 62 in 19 overs and Lillee 5 for 46 in 16.4 overs. Botham, who lost his middle stump for 1 to Alderman in the first innings, made top score of 33 in something more like his old manner. The Australians fielded and caught superbly, Yallop taking a memorable catch in the gully to remove Gooch.

Australia, in the best weather of the match, had some uneasy moments, but by the time Dilley returned to take four quick wickets they were almost there.

ENGLAND: First Innings

G. A. Gooch, c Wood, b Lillee	10
G. Boycott, c Border, b Alderman	27
R. A. Woolmer, c Wood, b Lillee	0
D. I. Gower, c Yallop, b Lillee	26
M. W. Gatting, lbw, b Hogg	52
P. Willey, c Border, b Alderman	10
I. T. Botham, b Alderman	1
P. R. Downton, c Yallop, b Alderman	8
G. R. Dilley, b Hogg	34
R. G. D. Willis, c Marsh, b Hogg	0
M. Hendrick, not out	6
Extras (lb 6, w 1, nb 4)	11
TOTAL	185

Fall of Wickets: 1–13, 2–13, 3–57, 4–67, 5–92, 6–96, 7–116, 8–159, 9–159, 10–185.

Bowling: Lillee, 13–3–34–3; Alderman, 24–7–68–4; Hogg, 11.4–1–47–3; Lawson, 8–3–25–0.

AUSTRALIA: First Innings

G. M. Wood, lbw, b Dilley	0
J. Dyson, c Woolmer, b Willis	5
G. N. Yallop, b Hendrick	13
K. J. Hughes, lbw, b Willis	7
T. M. Chappell, b Hendrick	17
A. R. Border, c and b Botham	63
R. W. Marsh, c Boycott, b Willis	19
G. F. Lawson, c Gower, b Botham	14
D. K. Lillee, c Downton, b Dilley	12
R. M. Hogg, c Boycott, b Dilley	0
T. M. Alderman, not out	12
Extras (b 4, lb 8, w 1, nb 4)	17
TOTAL	179

Fall of Wickets: 1–0, 2–21, 3–21, 4–33, 5–64, 6–89, 7–110, 8–147, 9–153, 10–179.

Bowling: Dilley, 20–7–38–3; Willis, 30–14–47–3; Hendrick, 20–7–43–2; Botham, 16.5–6–34–2.

ENGLAND: Second Innings

G. A. Gooch, c Yallop, b Lillee	6
G. Boycott, c Marsh, b Alderman	4
R. A. Woolmer, c Marsh, b Alderman	0
D. I. Gower, c sub, b Lillee	28
M. W. Gatting, lbw, b Alderman	15
P. Willey, lbw, b Lillee	13
I. T. Botham, c Border, b Lillee	33
P. R. Downton, lbw, b Alderman	3
G. R. Dilley, c Marsh, b Alderman	13
R. G. D. Willis, c Chappell, b Lillee	1
M. Hendrick, not out	0
Extras (lb 8, nb 1)	9
TOTAL	125

Fall of Wickets: 1–12, 2–12, 3–13, 4–39, 5–61, 6–94, 7–109, 8–113, 9–125, 10–125.

Bowling: Lillee, 16.4–2–46–5; Alderman, 19–3–62–5; Hogg, 3–1–8–0.

AUSTRALIA: Second Innings

J. Dyson, c Downton, b Dilley	38
G. M. Wood, c Woolmer, b Willis	8
G. N. Yallop, c Gatting, b Botham	6
K. J. Hughes, lbw, b Dilley	22
T. M. Chappell, not out	20
A. R. Border, b Dilley	20
R. W. Marsh, lbw, b Dilley	0
G. F. Lawson, not out	5
Extras (b 1, lb 6, nb 6)	13
TOTAL (6 wkts)	132

D. K. Lillee, R. M. Hogg and T. M. Alderman did not bat.

Fall of Wickets: 1–20, 2–40, 3–77, 4–80, 5–122, 6–122.

Bowling: Dilley, 11.1–4–24–4; Willis, 13–2–28–1; Hendrick, 20–7–33–0; Botham, 10–1–34–1.

Umpires: W. E. Alley and D. J. Constant.

Australia won by 4 wkts.

LEFT On a cloudy, humid morning Lillee, in the soon-to-become familiar headband that gave him the appearance of something between a wounded soldier and a Wimbledon veteran, cut the ball off the seam in the old, devastating fashion.

Woolmer, balletically caught here by Wood at first slip for nought, was also out for nought in the second innings, caught at the wicket off Alderman. He failed at Lord's, too, and that was the end of him.

BELOW The Australian glee was understandable, for England were now 13 for 2, with five more catches off the fast bowlers to come, all of them between wicket-keeper and gully. Lillee, making the most of his status as a convalescent, made regular sorties to the pavilion after bowling to get a rub down and a dry shirt.

LEFT Boycott, third out and hard-hatted, is caught by Border to give Alderman his first Test wicket. Not until his penultimate innings of the series, when he made 137 at the Oval, did Boycott assert himself, no matter how long he was at the wicket. Marsh looks as if he could have swallowed the ball himself.

BELOW Botham, head cocked as if listening for the first cuckoo and demonstrably pushing across the line, does not need to look round. Rumour has it he's been bowled and Marsh leaves him in no doubt about it. In the mood,

Botham's batting always has a dangerous edge to it, exhilaration, grandeur, a whiff of brutality. At other times, like here, he comes and goes quietly, accepting the inevitable.

LEFT Gatting, squat, round-faced, bearded, scowling, has the appearance of a minor character in Shakespeare, Bardolph say, or Pistol. He has, too, a similar ebullience. Quick to retaliate after mistakes, he drives aggressively through the covers, hooks punishingly, comes dancing down the pitch to the spinners (though he had few chances for this in these Tests). He made fifties in the first two Tests and another at the Oval, but was unable to get beyond them.

Nevertheless, there was always something refreshing about the sight of him striding to the wicket, as if no quarter would be asked or given. The best of him surely lies ahead.

RIGHT There's not much sign of strain about Botham as he rushes up to Hendrick. Yallop has just played Hendrick on to his stumps and Australia are 21 for 3. Gooch follows up behind like a copper in expressionless and dogged pursuit.

Hendrick, apart from taking 4 for 82 in Australia's second innings at the Oval, usually promised more than he achieved. Injury, misfortune in beating the bat continually without finding the edge, a tendency to bowl a shade short at crucial moments, have all combined to make Hendrick a less formidable bowler than he ought to be. He has a beautifully relaxed and high action, at a little above the pace at which Appleyard was such an effective bowler for Yorkshire and England in the 1950s.

LEFT Willis bowled well enough at Nottingham, especially on the first evening, without quite suggesting the devilish performances that were to follow. His stallionish pawing of the ground at the start of his run, the high-stepping, surf-breaking approach, the final teeth-gritting struggle, like an old bi-plane in a headwind, to get airborne – these sometimes come to nought, at others, like at Headingley, result in devastating lift. Always the eyes, under the rich helmet of hair, betoken unsung mysteries, trance-like absorbtion.

BELOW LEFT Willis's 200th Test wicket, with the penultimate ball of the last over of the first day. Hughes, Australia's captain, looks suitably thoughtful. Australia, 33 for 4, had lost much of the initiative gained by bowling England out for 185. Hughes was lbw in the second innings, and a few more times after that.

ABOVE RIGHT Border, dropped by Downton at 10 off Hendrick, went on to make 63, the highest and most crucial innings of the match. This was a beautiful ball, committing Border to the stroke and leaving him. It went straight into Downton's gloves as he moved across and straight out, suspiciously as though he was about to throw it up.

RIGHT Border, in the same innings, edges Willis between Botham and Gooch. Botham, generally the safest of slip fielders, put down Border at second slip when he was 17. Gooch and Dilley dropped two more comfortable slip catches before the day was over. Border, small, hairbrush-moustached, quick-footed, showed in this innings the tenacity that stood him in good stead through the series. Nearer in build and manner to Neil Harvey than, say, Arthur Morris or Bill Lawry among post-war Australian left-handers, he has much of Harvey's defensive resourcefulness.

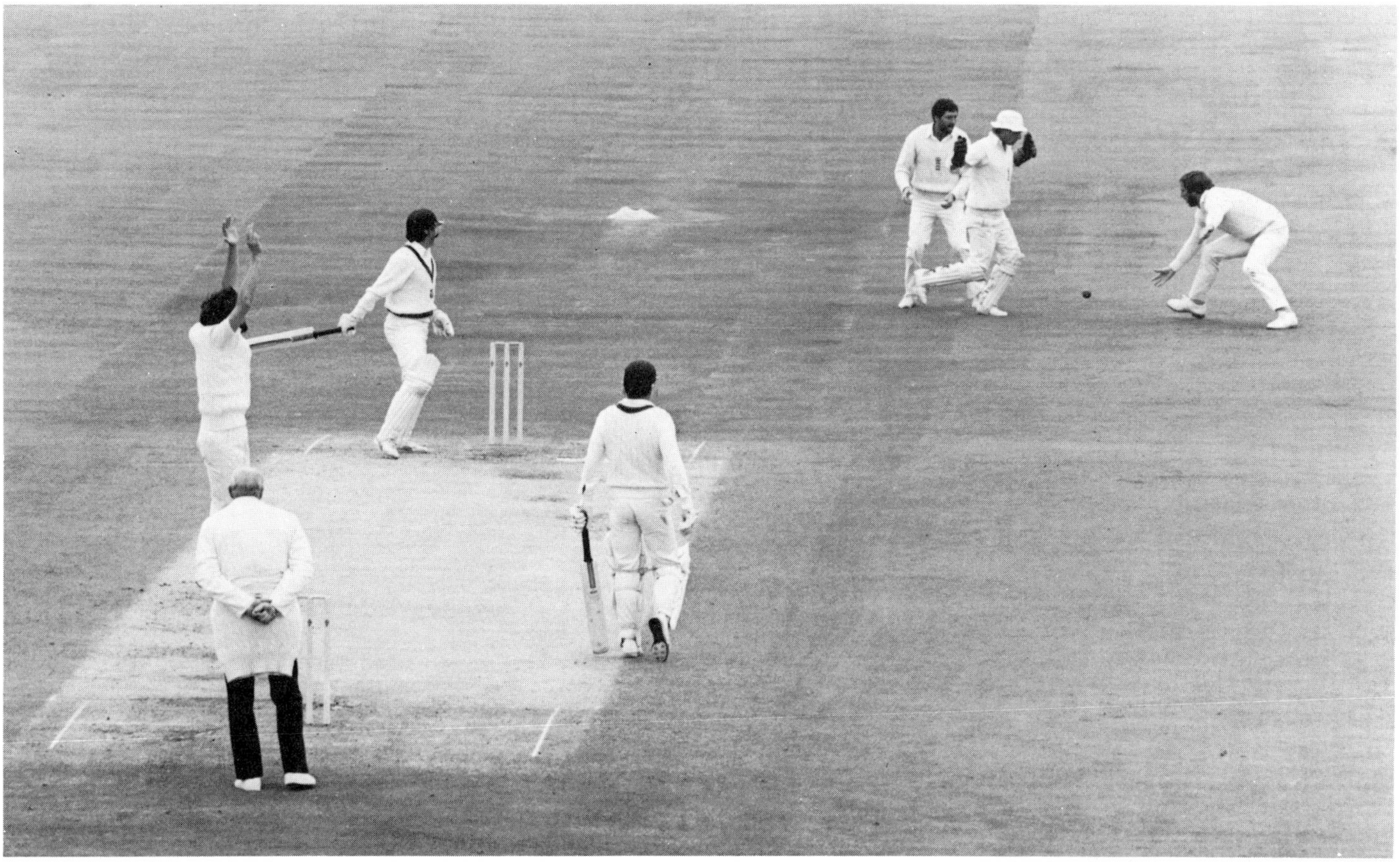

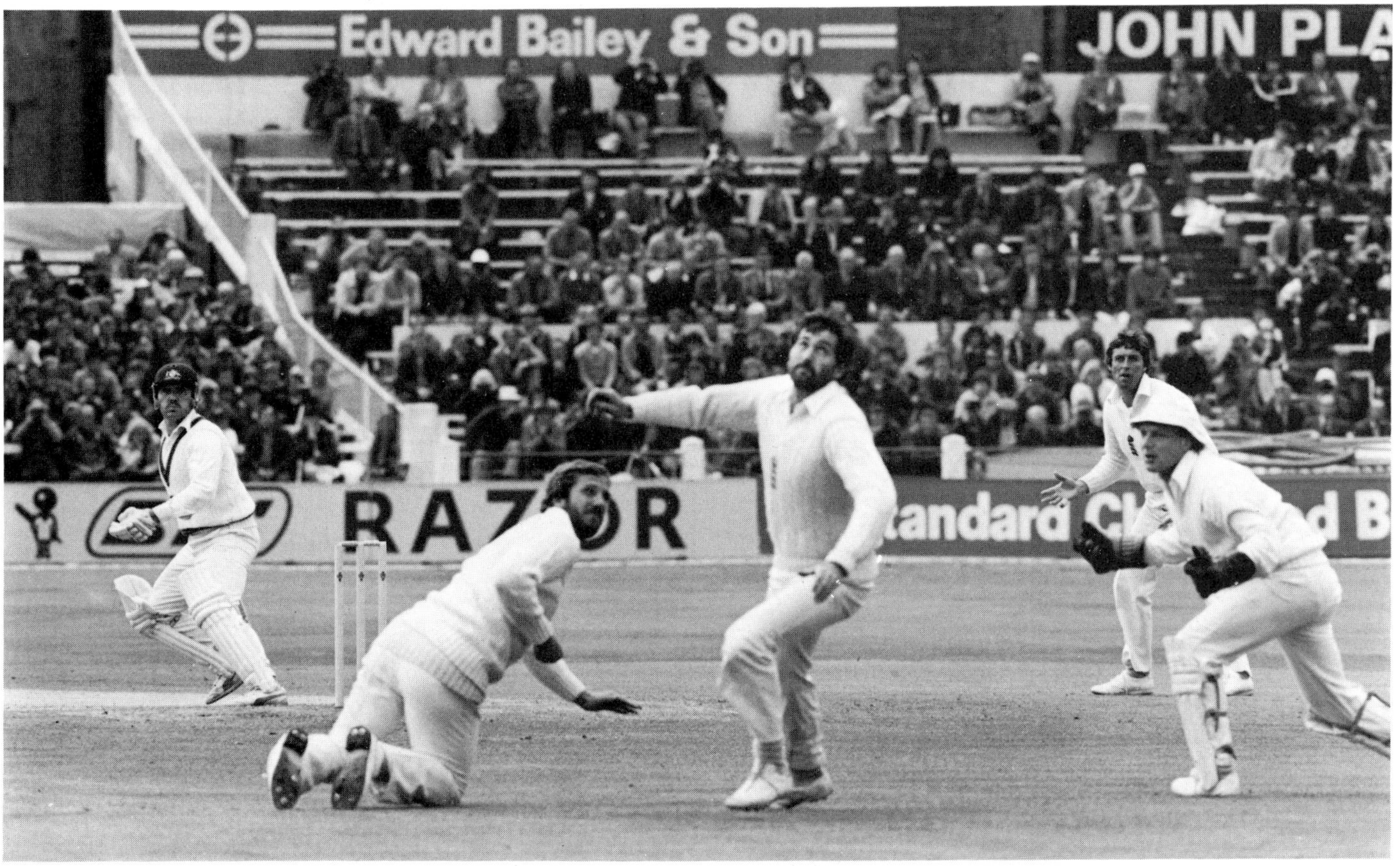
Edward Bailey & Son
JOHN PLA

Alderman gets Boycott cheaply for the second time in the match, the fielders' jubilance indication of relief at so prized a capture. As the series went on Boycott's wicket became less of an event, but the Australians never failed to show their pleasure at seeing the back of him. The stroke is

rigidly orthodox but the ball has moved off the pitch to take the edge. If some of the gestures suggest requests to be excused others are properly ecstatic, on this occasion perhaps with more justification than on others.

Woolmer bags a pair, the victim both times of particularly nasty deliveries. Would it have carried to first slip? Alderman is not likely to care. For Woolmer the opening bars of his swan song could faintly be heard. Marsh might either be pouncing on a rabbit or training for *L'Après-Midi d'un Faune*. His agility throughout was astonishing for so apparently earthbound a figure.

Yallop takes the catch of the match in the gully. Neither Gooch, the victim, nor Yallop, the catcher, are much in evidence. The rest are like bees in a swarm or observers of a fatality. Lillee smells honey.

LEFT Botham has just been caught by Border, low to his left at second slip, for 33. Lillee, delighted, points the way. Lillee, still not fully recovered from his infection and sweating profusely, bowled beautifully to take 5 for 46. None of the England bowlers, with the possible exception of Hendrick, found the length for this unreliable pitch to the same degree as Lillee and Alderman, who finished with 8 for 80 and 9 for 130 respectively.

ABOVE Botham's joy, at tea on the last day, is not unconfined. The match has all but been lost, though Dilley, too late, took four cheap wickets.

Marsh lbw bowled Dilley 0. But Australia, 122 for 6, need only 10 runs to win. Dilley, in two spells, removed Dyson, Hughes, Border and Marsh. The ball was still moving and at moments Dilley achieved real pace. At Headingley Dilley's batting and catching were crucial, but as the summer progressed the violent brake before his delivery stride seemed to lead him into all sorts of trouble, both of length and direction. His back and his legs seem to belong to two different people or to have been joined together without proper care and attention.

Gooch, with arms raised behind the stumps, had less and less to cheer about. Dropped for the Oval Test he took it out on county bowlers in a fashion that, sadly, he never approached for England.

England dropped catches to the last, Dyson, top scorer with 38, being put down at short leg by Woolmer when he was 16. Dyson, an elegant and correct player, failed at Lord's but carried the Australian first innings at Headingley, making his maiden Test century. Yet he, like Woolmer, was dropped before the series was out.

Trevor Chappell scores the winning run. He, too, had lost his place by Old Trafford, the shadows lengthening for him as also for Dilley and Downton. Botham and Gooch seem intent on preserving something from the match, if only their manhood.

For England, defeated ingloriously in the one-day Prudential Trophy, it was a depressing start to what most people hoped might be a happier season. This time it was the bowlers and fielders as much as the batsmen who failed. No one thought the pitch was of the quality for a Test match, though compared to those on which Nottinghamshire put in and shot out their opponents in county matches it was a batsman's paradise. Gatting and Gower flourished briefly in their familiar fashion in England's second innings, but it was the technique and application of Border that set the match up for Australia.

This was Botham's eleventh Test match as captain of England and he had won none of them. He was immediately reappointed to captain England at Lord's, though not for the rest of the series. Boycott was canvassed in *The Times* to take his place, as elsewhere were Knight, Fletcher and, less ardently, Brearley. It was Brearley before he retired who wanted Botham to succeed him and any such moves, involving much older players, would inevitably have seemed regressive. None of the current side, Willis, Gower, Gooch, seemed ideal, for one reason or another.

Downright ragged as England had looked at moments in the field it was not due to blunders of captaincy that they had lost. Lacking were the spark of Botham's own wayward genius and the sense of being tactically in control, regardless of the situation, that the best captains always exude.

SECOND TEST

LORD'S (2–7 July)

Test. Lord's weather tends to be either marvellous for Test matches or vile, sometimes both in the same match.

This time it was less than monsoon-like but generally depressing. The light on the first day was gloomy until the evening, bad enough for play to be stopped after lunch. On the second day four hours were lost, such play as there was being repeatedly interrupted, if not by showers then by drinks. When Lord's was eventually bathed in sunshine at seven o'clock the umpires decided, though an extra hour had been allocated, that it was time to go home.

In the circumstances it was perhaps surprising that the match, so slow getting under way, even approached a decision. But, belatedly, on the last afternoon, Botham was able to declare, setting Australia 232 to win. For most of the morning England were only too thankful to be climbing out of danger on the backs of Boycott and Gower. After lunch, however, they went for the runs, losing 5 wickets for 68. Australia lost 3 wickets for 17 – Dyson, Yallop, Hughes – but there was never really much likelihood of England bowling them out in three hours or of Australia going for the runs.

Hughes, winning the toss, had put England in. Gooch made 44 out of an opening partnership of 60 with Boycott, driving dismissively until he mishit a hook off Lawson. Gatting made 59 spiritedly and well before being leg-before to Bright ten minutes before the end. Lawson, much the fastest and most hostile of Australia's bowlers, took 3 for 40 as against Lillee's 0 for 76 and Alderman's 0 for 38. England finished the day at 191 for 4, Woolmer having retired hurt after being hit on the left arm by Lawson.

England were all out for 311, Willey accelerating nicely to make 82 but Emburey, sent in as night watchman, spending three hours over 31.

Australia lost four wickets for 81, but solid batting most of the way down – Wood 44, Hughes 42, Border 64, Marsh 47, Bright 33, Lillee 40 not out – took them into a lead of 39. But with only one day left England ended up 95 ahead and 8 wickets in hand. A draw was inevitable.

ENGLAND: First Innings

G. A. Gooch, c Yallop, b Lawson 44
G. Boycott, c Alderman, b Lawson 17
R. A. Woolmer, c Marsh, b Lawson 21
D. I. Gower, c Marsh, b Lawson 27
M. W. Gatting, lbw, b Bright 59
P. Willey, c Border, b Alderman 82
J. E. Emburey, run out 31
I. T. Botham, lbw, b Lawson 0
R. W. Taylor, c Hughes, b Lawson 0
G. R. Dilley, not out 7
R. G. D. Willis, c Wood, b Lawson 5
Extras (b 2, lb 3, w 3, nb 10) 18
TOTAL 311

Fall of Wickets: 1–60, 2–65, 3–134, 4–187, 5–284, 6–293, 7–293, 8–293, 9–298, 10–311.

Bowling: Lillee, 35.4–7–102–0; Alderman, 30.2–7–79–1; Lawson, 43.1–14–81–7; Bright, 15–7–31–1.

AUSTRALIA: First Innings

G. M. Wood, c Taylor, b Willis 44
J. Dyson, c Gower, b Botham 7
G. N. Yallop, b Dilley 1
K. J. Hughes, c Willis, b Emburey 42
T. M. Chappell, c Taylor, b Dilley 2
A. R. Border, c Gatting, b Botham 64
R. W. Marsh, lbw, b Dilley 47
R. J. Bright, lbw, b Emburey 33
G. F. Lawson, lbw, b Willis 5
D. K. Lillee, not out 40
T. M. Alderman, c Taylor, b Willis 5
Extras (b 6, lb 11, w 6, nb 32) 55
TOTAL 345

Fall of Wickets: 1–62, 2–62, 3–69, 4–81, 5–167, 6–244, 7–257, 8–268, 9–314, 10–345.

Bowling: Willis, 27.4–9–50–3; Dilley, 30–8–106–3; Botham, 26–8–71–2; Gooch, 10–4–28–0; Emburey, 25–12–35–2.

ENGLAND: Second Innings

G. A. Gooch, lbw, b Lawson 20
G. Boycott, c Marsh, b Lillee 60
R. A. Woolmer, lbw, b Alderman 9
D. I. Gower, c Alderman, b Lillee 89
M. W. Gatting, c Wood, b Bright 16
I. T. Botham, b Bright 0
P. Willey, c Chappell, b Bright 12
G. R. Dilley, not out 27
R. W. Taylor, b Lillee 9
Extras (b 2, lb 8, nb 13) 23
TOTAL (8 wkts dec) 265

J. E. Emburey and R. G. D. Willis did not bat.

Fall of Wickets: 1–31, 2–35, 3–178, 4–217, 5–217, 6–217, 7–242, 8–265.

Bowling: Lillee, 26.4–8–82–3; Alderman, 17–2–42–1; Lawson, 19–6–51–1; Bright, 36–18–67–3.

AUSTRALIA: Second Innings

G. M. Wood, not out 62
J. Dyson, lbw, b Dilley 1
G. N. Yallop, c Botham, b Willis 3
K. J. Hughes, lbw, b Dilley 4
T. M. Chappell, c Taylor, b Botham 5
A. R. Border, not out 12
Extras (w 1, nb 2) 3
TOTAL (4 wkts) 90

R. W. Marsh, R. J. Bright, G. F. Lawson, D. K. Lillee and T. M. Alderman did not bat.

Fall of Wickets: 1–2, 2–11, 3–17, 4–62.

Bowling: Willis, 12–3–35–1; Dilley, 7.5–1–18–2; Emburey, 21–10–24–0; Botham, 8–3–10–1.

Umpires: D. O. Oslear and K. E. Palmer.

Match drawn.

Boycott goes out to bat in his 100th Test. Gooch, close as a bodyguard, looks less than enchanted as Boycott doffs his helmet to the crowd.

LEFT Kim Hughes with his cap characteristically perched. By the end of the Edgbaston Test he must have wanted to shut the whole world out with it. Hughes only fleetingly suggested the dazzling hero of the Lord's Centenary Test when he made 117 and 84 in a style indicative of a new star. So often he got started only to get out on the brink of fluency. Boyish and unassertive as captain he was never dull; the Australian batting sometimes was, largely because he was rarely there long enough to put a proper gloss on it. In the absence of Greg Chappell no one else had quite the class or the brilliance to demolish an attack.

ABOVE Woolmer, heavily bandaged, but ready to bat on, watches play with Willey. Both had gone by Old Trafford, Woolmer inevitably, Willey a shade unluckily. If Woolmer has, since his return, seemed increasingly a shadow of his pre-Packer self, it is perhaps a sacrifice on the altar of security. Willey, despite glaring faults of technique, especially against spin, has usually made the most of his chances.

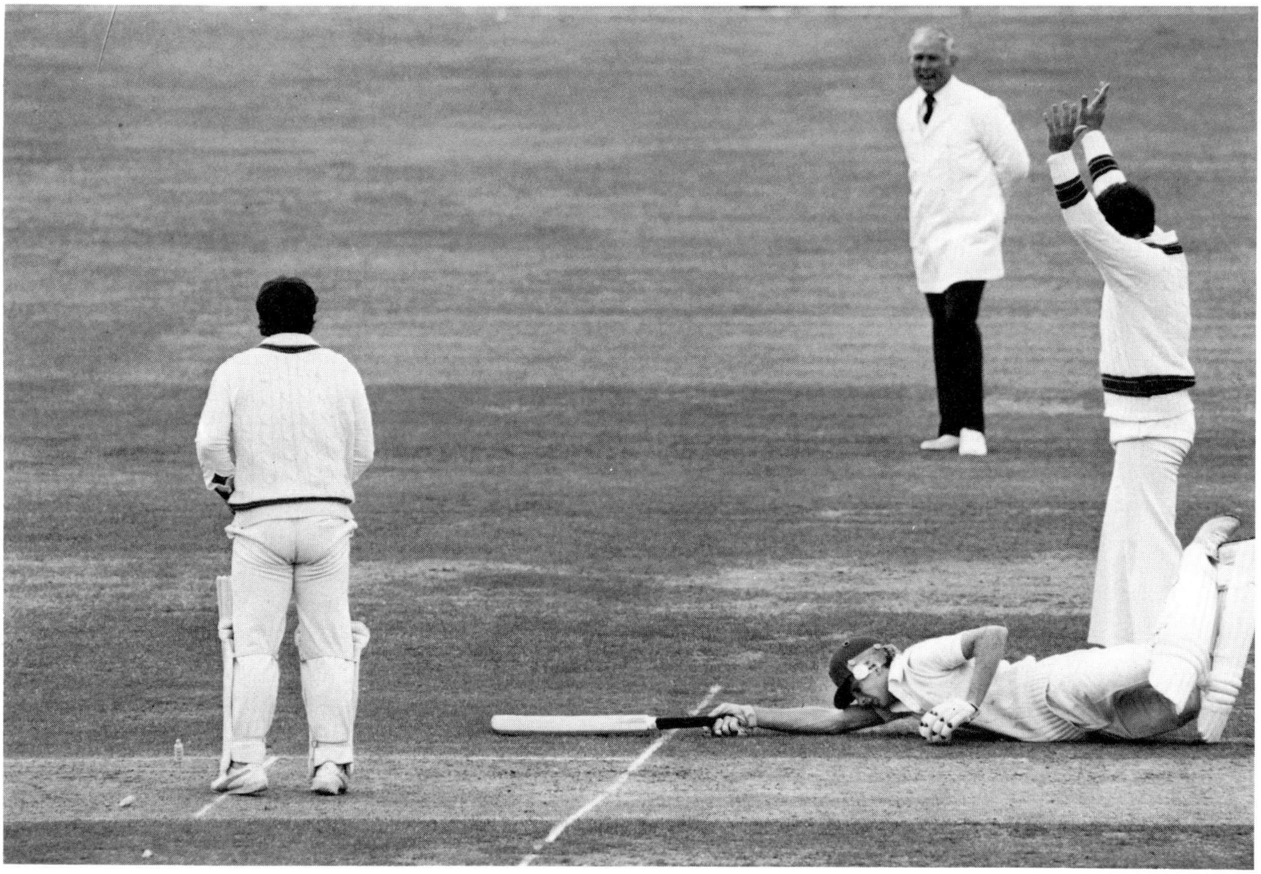

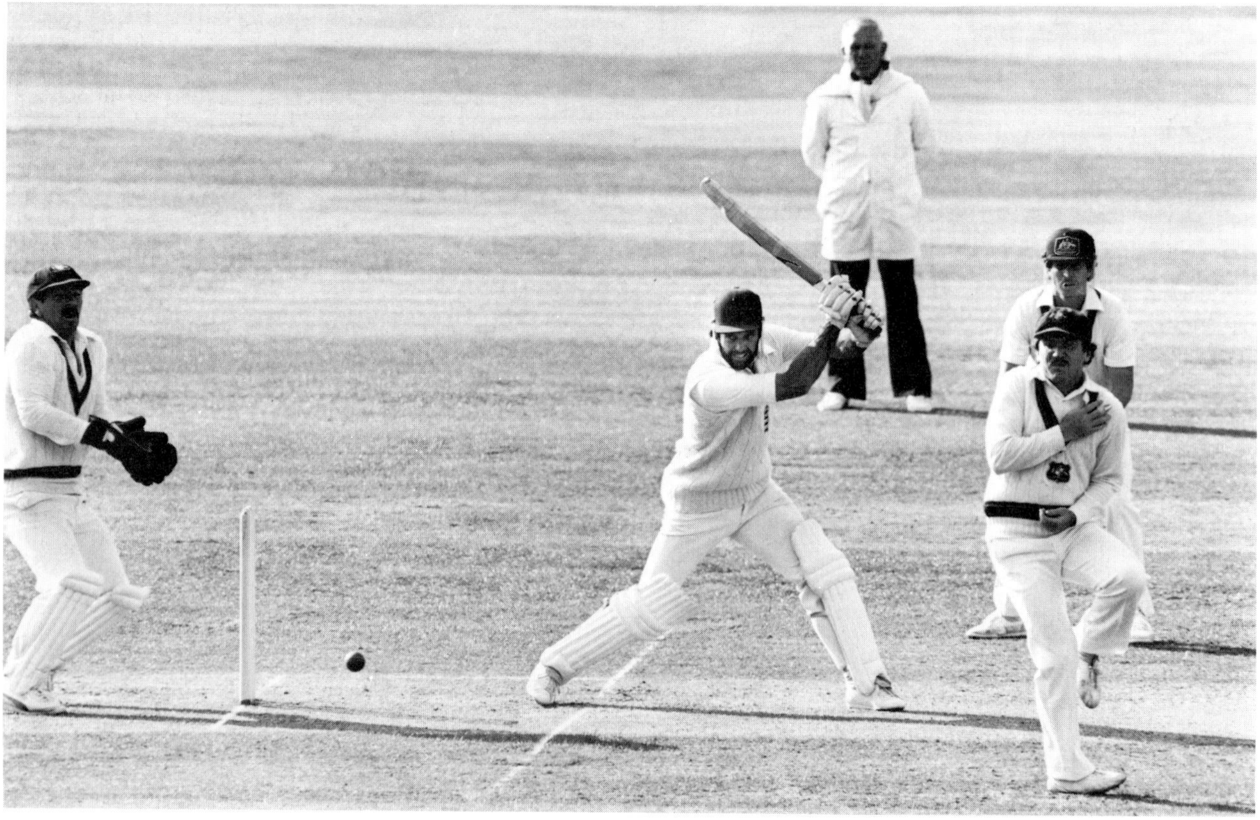

LEFT Gower, then 11, adjudged to have just beaten Lawson's throw from long-leg, though the Australians, some thought with good reason, felt differently.

BELOW LEFT Willey driving, Border pirouetting. Willey's open-shouldered stance does not prevent him from cover driving from a correct position, even if he does not start in one.

RIGHT Botham, delayed by Emburey's obduracy, has to come in at No. 8 and is leg-before to Lawson's third ball, out to an impatient stroke. England at this stage were in the process of going from 284 for 4 to 298 for 9.

BELOW Taylor picked up by Hughes at short leg off Lawson for nought. While Lillee was taking 0 for 102 and Alderman 1 for 79, Lawson took all the honours with 7 for 81. His form, as with Massie, another sensational performer at Lord's, did not fully hold up and injury kept him out of the last three Tests.

Leonardo drew anatomical
diagrams like these, expressive
as they are of tension and power.

Both Lawson, *left*, and Dilley
have left arms high, bodies
braced. From these pictures it is

impossible to see who is more
sideways on, but certainly it is
Lawson. Dilley's long back forms

an altogether less natural angle to his trunk. Where Lawson gains is in gathering momentum; Dilley has checked and his actual delivery is a secondary and considered movement, not an inevitable conclusion.

LEFT Wood magnificently caught
by Taylor off Willis for 44. The
ball flew off the inside edge and
Taylor, moving one way, had to
fling himself the other. Australia
lost this, their first wicket, at 62;
half an hour later, at lunch, they
were 81 for 4. Wood, who, like
Hughes, had made a fine hundred
in the Centenary Test, was
setting about the bowlers to the
extent that Dyson had made only
seven of the opening partnership.
No-balls predictably contributed
more.

RIGHT Border pulling Emburey
during his innings of 64. There is
no waste space about Border. He
capitalises on his chunkiness,
nose low to the ground.

BELOW Marsh cutting, Gatting
trucking; so close do short-leg
and silly mid-off squat for bat and
pad snicks that they have no
earthly chance of seeing the ball
off a genuine hit. All they can do
then is turn their backs and pray.

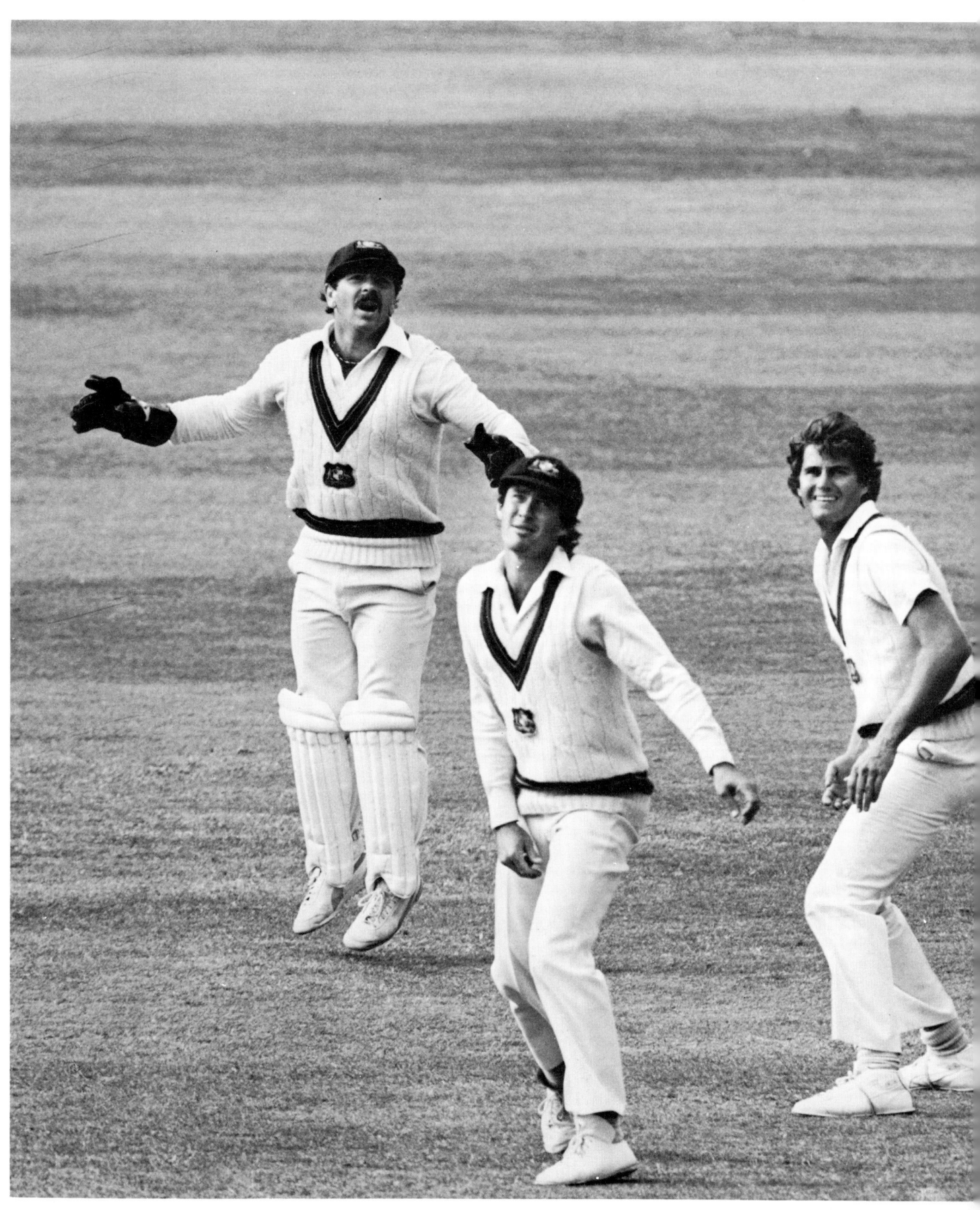

The Australian slips, more sharply angled than the habitual gentle arc of their English counterparts, watch one of Gower's airier strokes fly over them. There were many fine catches taken here and by Yallop at gully. In this picture Wood is at first slip, Border second, Alderman flashing his Pepsodent-white teeth at third, Dyson at fourth. So long as Gower was batting they never needed to be bored.

ABOVE Nothing flashy about this forward stroke of Boycott's, of a text-book correctness never wearying to its perpetrator, no matter how often repeated.

LEFT Botham, at the lowest point of his fortunes, bowled round his legs first ball by Bright. This was his second nought of the match, of no great consequence in itself as England were shortly to declare. Marsh looks almost embarrassed, Botham disbelieving. Botham returned to the pavilion in audible silence. 'The walk back,' he said later, 'seemed to grow longer and longer. It was like taking two steps forward and one step back.'

RIGHT Gower lofting Bright wide of mid-on during his innings of 89. Bright, bowling over the wicket into the bowler's rough, caused Gower plenty of trouble.

The shadows lengthening and England, in the dying moments, holding the initiative for the first time in the match. With eight wickets in hand on the last evening Australia had to hold out for two hours. Hughes soon went, leg-before to Dilley, and, before the end, Chappell. But there was no real danger and nothing came the way of these seven pairs of hands.

No sooner had the match ended than Botham informed the Selectors that he no longer wished to be considered as captain on the present one-match basis. Brearley was approached the same evening and offered the captaincy. He accepted.

THIRD TEST

HEADINGLEY (16–21 July)

The weather, although it was now late July, showed no improvement. Cool and dark at the start – play was stopped in the second over for bad light – it was soon raining heavily. Nevertheless, at the end of a dour first day, in which England dropped three out of four catches, two by Botham, Australia had reached 203 for 3. Dyson, in his twenty-second Test innings, made his maiden Test century. England, in conditions ideal for swing bowling, bowled too short and too wide.

Australia, who had won the toss, declared at 401 for 9, Hughes making a restrained though handsome 89, Yallop a dogged 58. Botham took five wickets after tea to finish with 6 for 95.

England's extravagant wastefulness of an unreliable pitch and heavy atmosphere was soon emphasized by Lillee, Alderman and Lawson. Moving the ball considerably and often late, and cutting it both ways off the seam, they bowled England out for 174.

Lillee, on his 32nd birthday, took 5 wickets, pushing his total of Test wickets up to 267. Marsh, who took four catches, passed Knott's record of 263 Test dismissals when he caught Botham, typically, off Lillee. Sixty-three of Marsh's catches have come off the bowling of Lillee and he reached his target in 22 Tests less than Knott.

When Botham came out to bat a second time England were 103 for 5. They were soon 133 for 7, still 92 runs behind Australia and the end apparently in sight. At the close of play Botham was 145 not out, having been at the wicket only three hours and a half. He had hit 26 fours, and one six.

The last day, in its reversal of fortunes, turned out to be one of the most extraordinary in Test history. Australia, set the modest target of 130, were 56 for 1 shortly before lunch.

At 48 for 1, however, Willis had been allowed the Kirkstall Lane end and the breeze. The effect was immediate. He banged the ball into the pitch on or just short of a length and it reared up alarmingly. Chappell, protecting his head, was caught at the wicket, Hughes went for nought to a low catch by Botham at slip, Yallop was grabbed at forward short leg.

After lunch Old bowled Border, and Willis, thundering in, demolished the remainder. England had won by 18 runs, the first time a side following on had won a Test since 1894/5 when England, under A. E. Stoddart, beat Australia by 10 runs at Sydney.

AUSTRALIA: First Innings

J. Dyson, b Dilley 102
G. M. Wood, lbw, b Botham 34
T. M. Chappell, c Taylor, b Willey 27
K. J. Hughes, c and b Botham 89
R. J. Bright, b Dilley 7
G. N. Yallop, c Taylor, b Botham 58
A. R. Border, lbw, b Botham 8
R. W. Marsh, b Botham 28
G. F. Lawson, c Taylor, b Botham 13
D. K. Lillee, not out 3
Extras (b 4, lb 13, w 3, nb 12) 32

TOTAL (9 wkts dec) 401

T. M. Alderman did not bat.

Fall of Wickets: 1–55, 2–149, 3–196, 4–220, 5–332, 6–354, 7–357, 8–396, 9–401.

Bowling: Willis, 30–8–72–0; Old, 43–14–91–0; Dilley, 27–4–78–2; Botham, 38.2–11–95–6; Willey, 13–2–31–1; Boycott, 3–2–2–0.

ENGLAND: First Innings

G. A. Gooch, lbw, b Alderman 2
G. Boycott, b Lawson 12
J. M. Brearley, c Marsh, b Alderman 10
D. I. Gower, c Marsh, b Lawson 24
M. W. Gatting, lbw, b Lillee 15
P. Willey, b Lawson 8
I. T. Botham, c Marsh, b Lillee 50
R. W. Taylor, c Marsh, b Lillee 5
G. R. Dilley, c and b Lillee 13
C. M. Old, c Border, b Alderman 0
R. G. D. Willis, not out 1
Extras (b 6, lb 11, w 6, nb 11) 34

TOTAL 174

Fall of Wickets: 1–12, 2–40, 3–42, 4–84, 5–87, 6–112, 7–148, 8–166, 9–167, 10–174.

Bowling: Lillee, 18.5–7–49–4; Alderman, 19–4–59–3; Lawson, 13–3–32–3.

ENGLAND: Second Innings

G. A. Gooch, c Alderman, b Lillee 0
G. Boycott, lbw, b Alderman 46
J. M. Brearley, c Alderman, b Lillee 14
D. I. Gower, c Border, b Alderman 9
M. W. Gatting, lbw, b Alderman 1
P. Willey, c Dyson, b Lillee 33
I. T. Botham, not out 149
R. W. Taylor, c Bright, b Alderman 1
G. R. Dilley, b Alderman 56
C. M. Old, b Lawson 29
R. G. W. Willis, c Border, b Alderman 2
Extras (b 5, lb 3, w 3, nb 5) 16

TOTAL 356

Fall of Wickets: 1–0, 2–18, 3–37, 4–41, 5–105, 6–133, 7–135, 8–252, 9–319, 10–356.

Bowling: Lillee, 25–6–94–3; Alderman, 35.3–6–135–6; Lawson, 23–4–96–1; Bright, 4–0–15–0.

AUSTRALIA: Second Innings

J. Dyson, c Taylor, b Willis 34
G. M. Wood, c Taylor, b Botham 10
T. M. Chappell, c Taylor, b Willis 8
K. J. Hughes, c Botham, b Willis 0
G. N. Yallop, c Gatting, b Willis 0
A. R. Border, b Old 0
R. W. Marsh, c Dilley, b Willis 4
R. J. Bright, b Willis 19
G. F. Lawson, c Taylor, b Willis 1
D. K. Lillee, c Gatting, b Willis 17
T. M. Alderman, not out 0
Extras (lb 3, w 1, nb 14) 18

TOTAL 111

Fall of Wickets: 1–13, 2–56, 3–58, 4–58, 5–65, 6–68, 7–74, 8–75, 9–110, 10–111.

Bowling: Botham, 7–3–14–1; Dilley, 2–0–11–0; Willis, 15.1–3–43–8; Old, 9–1–21–1; Willey, 3–1–4–0.

Umpires: B. J. Meyer and D. G. Evans.

England won by 18 runs.

There was not much to laugh about on the first day. Seals might have been happier.

LEFT Historic matches have their casualties. Headingley 1981 will forever be associated with Botham's 149 not out and Willis's 8 for 43. But Dyson, a correct, elegant player, with a pleasant back foot cover drive, will remember it for his maiden Test century. He batted, save for the last half-hour, throughout a long day. It was, inevitably, a painstaking rather than a polished effort, for the ball was moving about and frequently finding the edge. At 57 Dyson was dropped in the gully off Dilley.

RIGHT Hughes is by nature an adventurous batsman, but in this long, dour innings of 89 he had to curb most of his attacking instincts. Almost unable to believe their good fortune in surviving in conditions ideal for England's four-man pace attack the Australians set about grinding out as many runs as they could. 401 was enough to make England follow-on but not, as it happened, to win the match. Hughes produced the occasional flashing stroke through the covers, but they were few and far between. Eleven short of his century and after batting for four and a half hours Hughes miscued a push to leg off Botham and gave the bowler a gentle return catch.

Brearley, sacrificially assuming the fatal No. 3 position, is caught by Marsh off Alderman after struggling for an hour. Gooch's repeated failure turned No. 3 into virtually an opening batsman, no novelty for Brearley, at least. If Brearley only twice in eight innings approached his county form his cool assurance and tactical sense in the field – quite apart from his evident

ability to get the best out of his players – transformed a losing side into a winning one. The rows of heads behind the wicket have always reminded me of a shooting gallery; if you hit one with a pot shot you feel it would immediately pop up again.

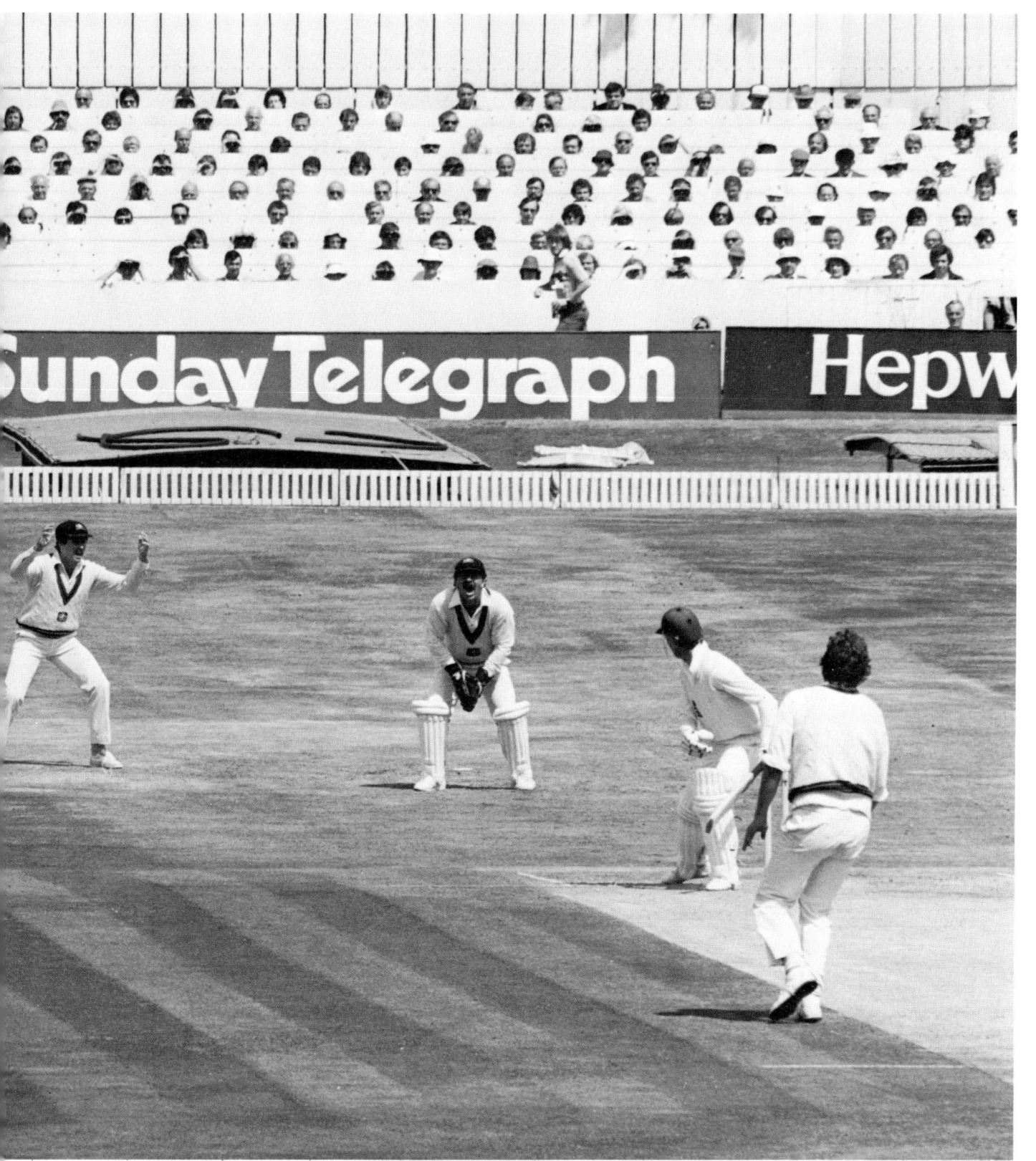

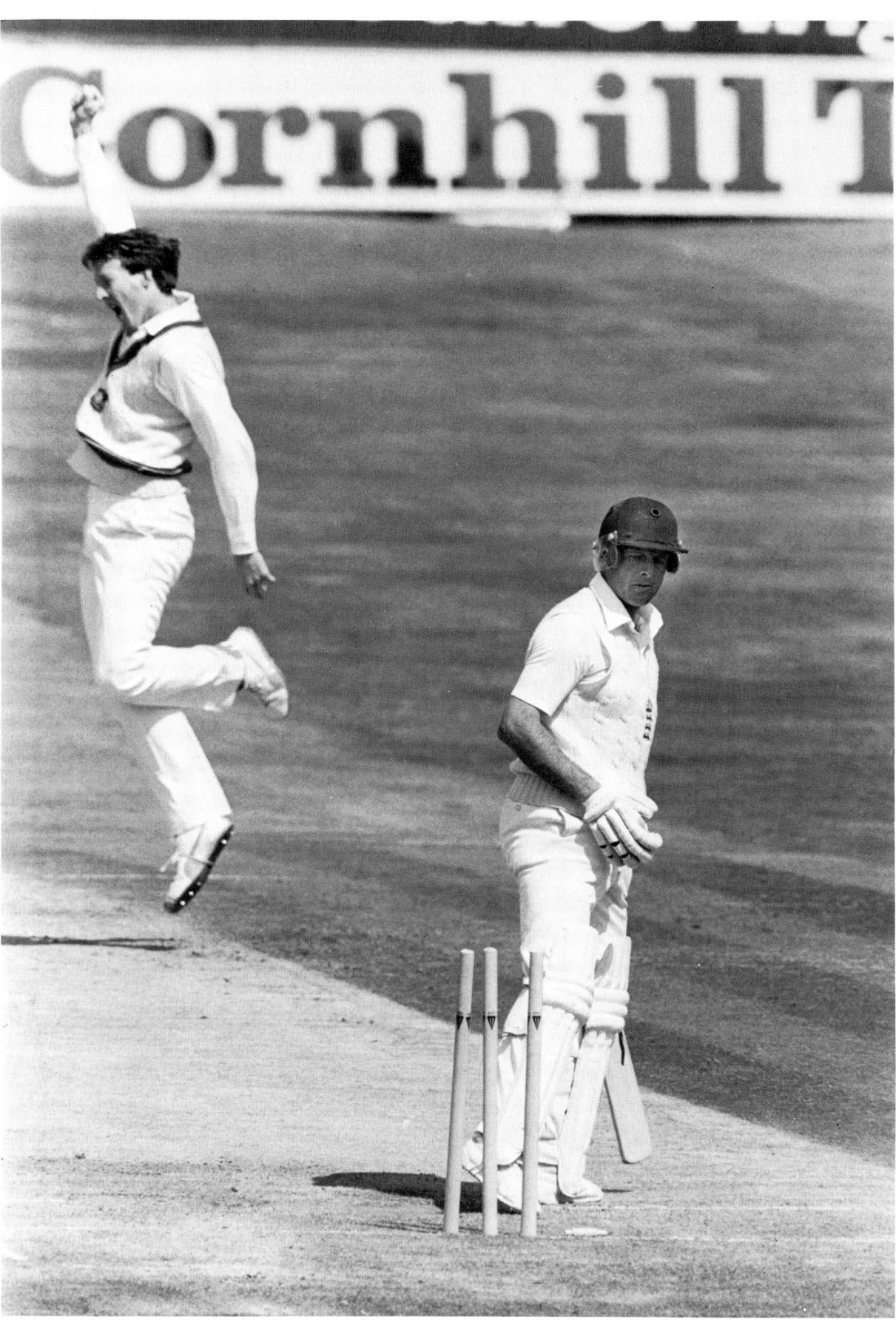

LEFT Lawson might well do a Highland fling for not all that many bowlers hit Boycott's stumps. Boycott had been batting 80 minutes for 12 and scarcely managed more than a prod. 27, 4, 17 and 60 were Boycott's scores up till then, none of them made in a manner to deflate the morale of the surging Australian fast bowlers. Still, he remained the best England had, and he emphasised it at the Oval. Lawson at Lord's, with his long-striding open action, something along the lines of McKenzie, had been much the fastest of the Australians. In this innings he took 3 for 32, twice hitting the stumps.

RIGHT It is hard to deny bowlers, captains, fielders expressing pleasure in success, but effusive-ness nowadays often goes too far. Hughes's and Lawson's delight is understandable here, but it is not uncommon in both Test and county matches to see bowlers being applauded by their colleagues for bowling a straight ball, or beating the bat, or achieving a maiden that has largely consisted of bouncers and near wides.

Photo: Eric Beecher

ABOVE LEFT Botham seems to be setting off to shoot rabbits, Marsh about to pitch in a baseball game, first slip to have spotted a U.F.O. In fact, Marsh has caught Botham off Lillee for 50 and become the most successful wicket-keeper in Test history. In this innings the first hints of Botham's renaissance became visible.

LEFT Lindwall once did this to Hutton, though Hutton was wearing a cap not a helmet. Hutton has remarked that in all his cricketing career, when he had quite as torrid a time as anyone since, he never expected to be hit on the head and only once was. Boycott has got out of the way all right, but the undignified posture is not unlike that of a drunken sailor or a copper after a heavy day in Brixton.

ABOVE Dilley's assault on the Australian bowling was the start of the fight back. His feet were often far from the ball but his long reach and the power of his strokes saved him. All three behind him have moustaches.

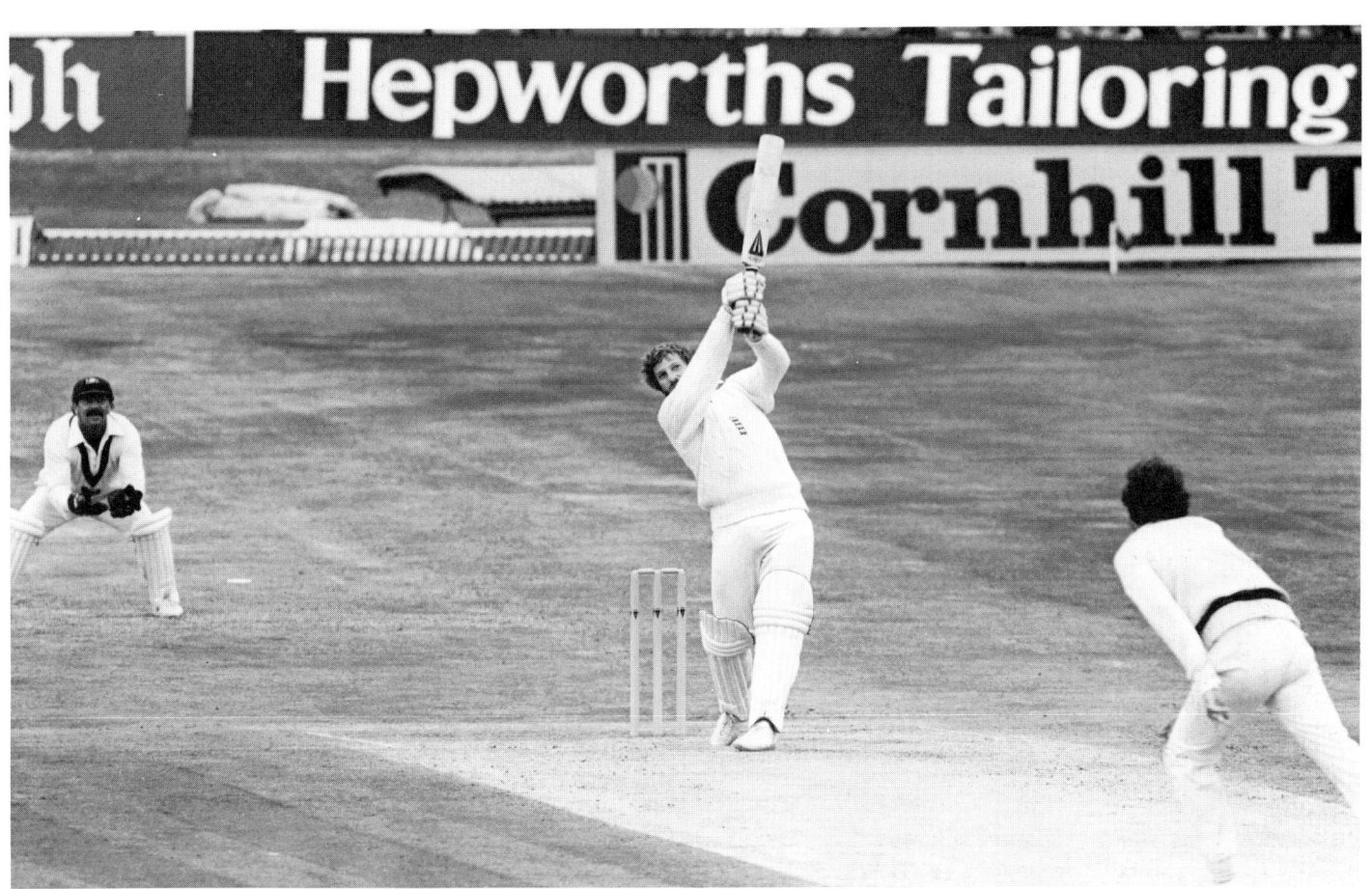

LEFT Botham's wolfish grin as he hooks Lawson tells its own tale. The hunter is back on the trail.

The transformation from a drawn, frowning and nail-biting figure to the buccaneering Botham of memory took a matter of two weeks. The smile returned. The bounciness reappeared in the run-up to the wicket, and with it extra pace and swing. Batting, Botham has always had an essentially correct technique, hitting straight and through the line of the ball. Now, in a situation where there was absolutely nothing to lose, he recaptured the confidence to let the bowlers have it.

ABOVE By the time Botham had hit the all-conquering Alderman back over his head for six the Australians were in some disarray. Botham's innings, discomforting as it was momentarily, nevertheless seemed at this stage more an indulgence than a threat.

LEFT Botham developed a fancy for hooking off his eyebrows. Once or twice, as at Old Trafford, he unnervingly looked to take his eyes off the ball, but the result was usually the same – four or six to long-leg. After a pair at Lord's, Botham's contribution at Headingley was 50 and 149 not out (to say nothing of 6 for 95, 1 for 14, and two catches).

ABOVE Small boys will remember touching their hero on his return all their lives. Old men up here can never have seen anything like it, except once before, by Botham, off a mild Indian attack. They are more used to Boycott in these parts and no fancy stuff before tea.

More often, southerners get a roasting up north. Ask Fletcher, or Graveney, or Compton. Only

Dexter in recent years has hit the ball with Botham's power, though Milburn, before his accident, and Barber, used to score at a great rate.

LEFT If ever a man deserved a banana it was Lillee. He may be losing his hair, he was only half-fit, but he never looked other than a magnificent bowler. The old pace was kept in reserve, but the hostility, the immaculate length and line, the late movement, were still there. Lillee in this series was less the demolishing fast bowler, the superb athlete, than the old fox, sniffing out weaknesses. At little over medium pace, and used discriminatingly, he was always a danger.

Lillee took his 142nd wicket against England when he had Willey caught at short third man. The previous record for Anglo-Australian Tests was held by the Australian off spinner, Hugh Trumble, with 141. Rhodes, with 109, holds the English record.

ABOVE Boycott surrounded. Yorkshiremen can do no wrong at Headingley in Tests, though Boycott has had his ups and downs, not least in county matters. Before the series finished he had become England's leading scorer in Test history, passing Cowdrey. A far cry, his present glossy appearance and urbane manner, from the bespectacled, silent and balding youth who took his first awkward steps on this ground twenty years ago.

Willis getting his own back for
the similar humiliation suffered
earlier by Boycott. Once Willis
had changed ends and begun to
dig the ball in the steepness of
his lift made it hard to control.

Hughes has taken his right
hand away here and seems
uncertain as to the result. He
lasted only a few balls, being
well caught by Botham at second
slip off Willis in the over before
lunch.

Yallop, too, went in this over for
nought. In this case the ball
reared off a length and Yallop,
fending it down, was splendidly
caught by Gatting at forward
short-leg. There was a split
second for Gatting to react and
he did.

The beginning of a stroke and the thankful end of it. Marsh hooks Willis high and hard off the meat of the bat and Dilley, a yard in from the boundary at long-leg, judges a beastly catch to perfection. Not for nothing did Brearley, Botham and Willey crowd round him, for Marsh could have won the match with a few blows. Bright at the other end and Lillee, replacing Lawson, added 35 in only four overs with calculated hitting, and it looked suddenly as if England's Herculean efforts would all be in vain.

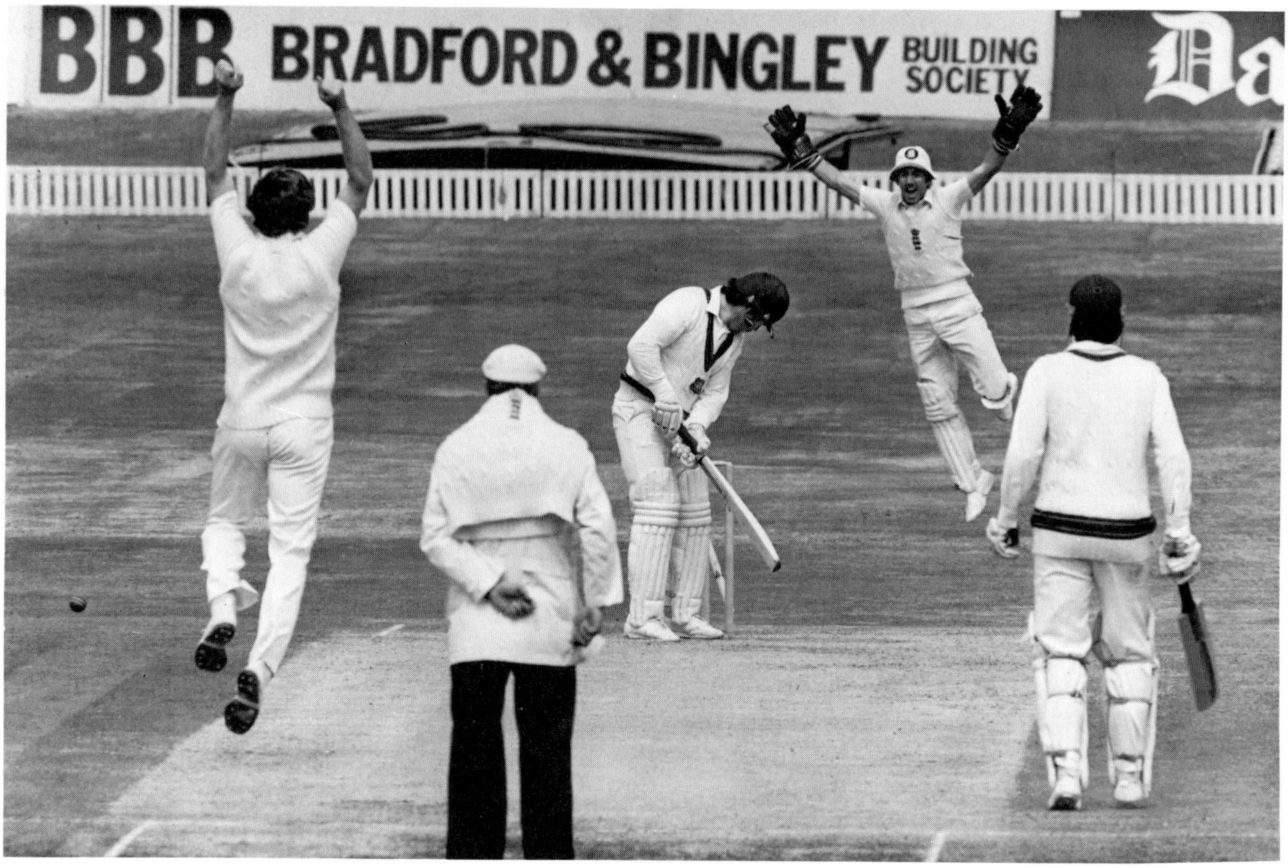
BBB BRADFORD & BINGLEY BUILDING SOCIETY

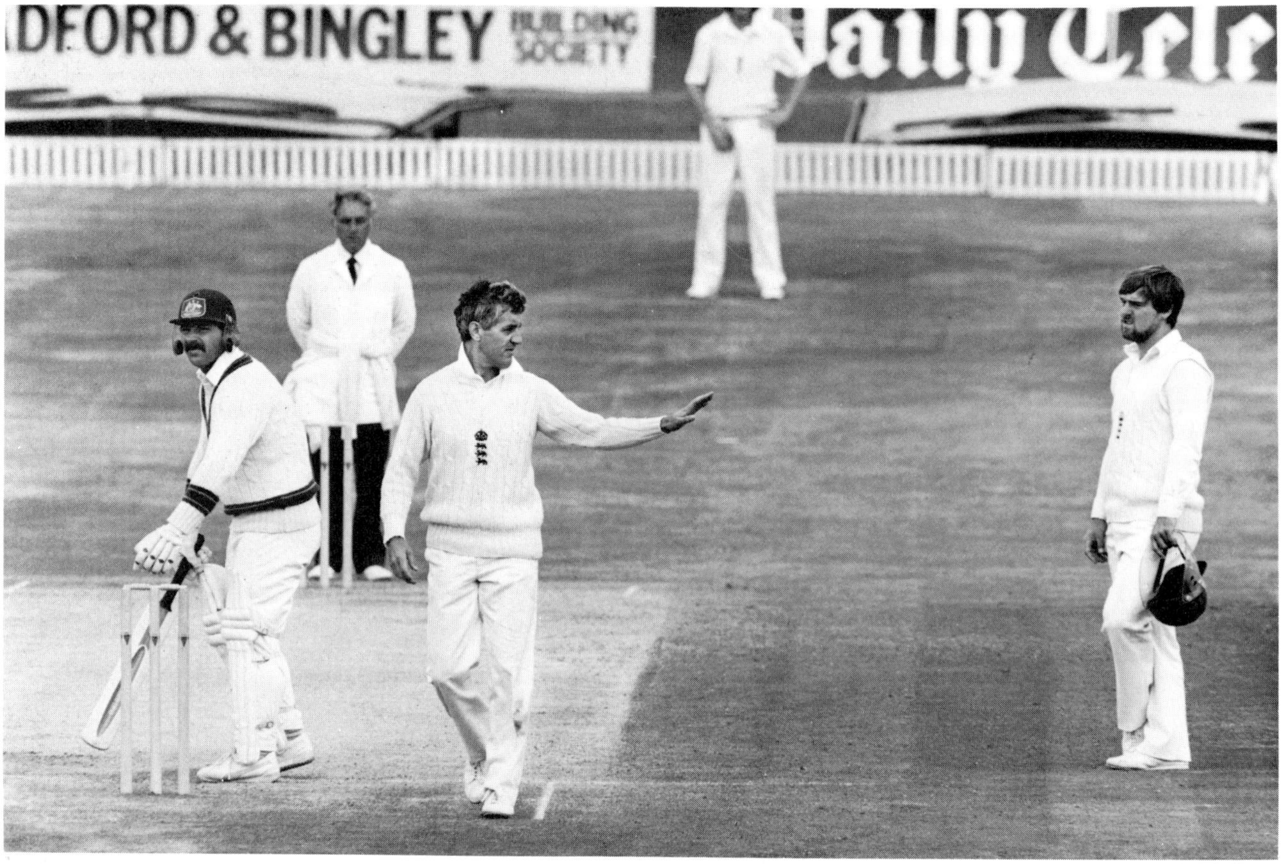
BUILDING SOCIETY

LEFT Border, so often the obstacle to English progress, bowled by Old for nought, the third duck in a row. After lunch Willis, far from stiffening up, tore in even more ferociously and Old, tearing out Border's leg stump with one that whipped back at him, opened up the tail. Old, not renowned for his staunchness against fast bowling, had made 29, putting on 67 with Botham, in England's second innings. As prey to injury as anyone who has ever played for England, Old's contribution to England's victory was invaluable. Newly bearded, he twice dropped Alderman at slip in the penultimate over of the match. Perhaps a whisker got in his eye. It was lucky he was not Fletcher. Injury prevented him playing in the last two Tests.

BELOW LEFT Not an admonishment from Brearley but advice, one imagines, to Gatting to keep his distance. Brearley's calm and collected ordering of his fielders, in nerve-wracking circumstances, was exemplary. Marsh seems to be warning Taylor to keep his hands off his wicket.

ABOVE RIGHT Lawson was soon on his way, following an outswinger from Willis into Taylor's safe gloves.

RIGHT Willis was not going to be apprehended, even by admiring supporters. He tore off the field as fast as he had run up to bowl. The beards of Gatting, Gooch and Willey open to disclose pearly-white teeth and delighted smiles. It is all over.

What had begun in rain and gloom ended in sunshine and euphorìa. If Mum was watching she must have been proud. In a month of winter weather, rising unemployment and inner-city riots a policeman was lucky to be drafted among this lot. The series, instead of being dead as a dormouse, as had seemed likely at the week-end, was now miraculously restored. The crowds would roll up in plenty for Edgbaston, Old Trafford and the Oval, and Willis's run to the wicket would be accompanied by roars and chanting of the kind usually heard only on a football field. English crowds had had little to shout about, one way and another, this summer but at last they had something to cheer. There was a Royal wedding coming up, too.

FOURTH TEST

EDGBASTON (30 July–4 August)

The hopes that England, on a lovely day and on a pitch expected to be packed with runs, would now get off to a decent start, soon went up in smoke. By the first evening, with England bowled out for a mere 189, the triumph of Headingley had dwindled into mirage. Alderman, once again, bowled excellently, taking 5 for 42. All but Gower of England's batsmen settled in, only to lose their wickets with careless or indifferent strokes. Few blows were struck in either anger or delight; mostly, it was an uphill trudge, devoid of distinction or character, on a slow, lifeless pitch.

Australia fared marginally better, taking most of the second day to establish a lead of 69 and then taking one English wicket for 49.

The Australians batted steadily if rarely entertainingly. As with England, most of them got off to a start only to lose their way in their twenties, thirties, or forties. Hughes, visibly put out by Willis's short-pitching, made 47, Kent, in his first Test innings, 46.

England, in their second innings, allowed themselves to be pinned down in humiliating fashion by the slow left arm of Bright. Bright finished with 5 for 68 in 34 overs, and most of the time he had fielders squatting close enough to England's leading batsmen for them to count the fillings in their teeth. However, Emburey, sweeping, and Taylor, scotching the spin, put on 50 together after Old had cowshotted Bright out of the attack. When they came together England were 167 for 8, a mere 98 ahead. Alderman took the last three wickets and Australia, with all the time in the world, needed only 150 to win.

Three wickets went down for 29, Wood lbw to a nasty one from Old, Dyson lbw to Willis, Hughes caught by Emburey off Willis. But Border, two hours over 11, and Yallop, two hours over 30, inched their way forwards. At lunch time on the Sunday, when most people were sitting down to their weekly joint, Australia were 62 for 3 and they had spent nearly forty overs at it.

They got to 87 before, first, Yallop went to a bat-pad catch off Emburey, and then Border, unable to avoid a brutish ball from Emburey that turned and lifted, was caught off his glove.

Brearley summoned up Botham and in minutes the match was over. Marsh lost his middle stump, Bright was lbw next ball, Lillee was caught at the wicket, Kent was bowled off his pads. Alderman came and went like a ghost. In 28 balls Botham had taken 5 wickets for 1 run and England were home, against all the odds, by 29 runs.

ENGLAND: First Innings

G. Boycott, c Marsh, b Alderman.......... 13
J. M. Brearley, c Border, b Lillee.......... 48
D. I. Gower, c Hogg, b Alderman.......... 0
G. A. Gooch, c Marsh, b Bright.. 21
M. W. Gatting, c Alderman, b Lillee.. 21
P. Willey, b Bright.................... 16
I. T. Botham, b Alderman.............. 26
J. E. Emburey, b Hogg................. 3
R. W. Taylor, b Alderman.............. 0
C. M. Old, not out.................... 11
R. G. D. Willis, c Marsh, b Alderman...... 13
Extras (b 1, lb 5, w 1, nb 10)........... 17
TOTAL....................189

Fall of Wickets: 1–29, 2–29, 3–60, 4–101, 5–126, 6–145, 7–161, 8–161, 9–165, 10–189.

Bowling: Lillee, 18–4–61–2; Alderman, 23.1–8–42–5; Hogg, 16–3–49–1; Bright, 12–4–20–2.

AUSTRALIA: First Innings

G. M. Wood, run out..................... 38
J. Dyson, b Old.... 1
A. R. Border, c Taylor, b Old............. 2
R. J. Bright, lbw, b Botham.............. 27
K. J. Hughes, lbw, b Old................. 47
G. N. Yallop, b Emburey................. 30
M. F. Kent, c Willis, b Emburey.......... 46
R. W. Marsh, b Emburey................. 2
D. K. Lillee, b Emburey................. 18
R. M. Hogg, run out.................... 0
T. M. Alderman, not out................. 3
Extras (b 4, lb 19, nb 21)............... 44
TOTAL....................258

Fall of Wickets: 1–5, 2–14, 3–62, 4–115, 5–166, 6–203, 7–220, 8–253, 9–253, 10–258.

Bowling: Willis, 19–3–63–0; Old, 21–8–44–3; Emburey, 26.5–12–43–4; Botham, 20–1–64–1.

ENGLAND: Second Innings

G. Boycott, c Marsh, b Bright.............. 29
J. M. Brearley, lbw, b Lillee.............. 13
D. I. Gower, c Border, b Bright............ 23
G. A. Gooch, b Bright.................... 21
M. W. Gatting, b Bright.................. 39
P. Willey, b Bright...................... 5
I. T. Botham, c Marsh, b Lillee............ 3
C. M. Old, c Marsh, b Alderman........... 23
J. E. Emburey, not out................... 37
R. W. Taylor, lbw, b Alderman............ 8
R. G. D. Willis, c Marsh, b Alderman....... 2
Extras (lb 6, w 1, nb 9).................. 16
TOTAL....................219

Fall of Wickets: 1–18, 2–52, 3–89, 4–98, 5–110, 6–116, 7–154, 8–167, 9–217, 10–219.

Bowling: Lillee, 26–9–51–2; Alderman, 22–5–65–3; Hogg, 10–3–19–0; Bright, 34–17–68–5.

AUSTRALIA: Second Innings

J. Dyson, lbw, b Willis.................. 13
G. M. Wood, lbw, b Old.................. 2
A. R. Border, c Gatting, b Emburey........ 40
K. J. Hughes, c Emburey, b Willis......... 5
G. N. Yallop, c Botham, b Emburey........ 30
M. F. Kent, b Botham.................... 10
R. W. Marsh, b Botham.................. 4
R. J. Bright, lbw, b Botham.............. 0
D. K. Lillee, c Taylor, b Botham.......... 3
R. M. Hogg, not out.................... 0
T. M. Alderman, b Botham............... 0
Extras (b 1, lb 2, nb 11)................. 14
TOTAL....................121

Fall of Wickets: 1–2, 2–19, 3–29, 4–87, 5–105, 6–114, 7–114, 8–120, 9–121, 10–121.

Bowling: Willis, 20–6–37–2; Old, 11–4–19–1; Emburey, 22–10–40–2; Botham, 14–9–11–5.

Umpires: H. D. Bird and D. O. Oslear.

England won by 29 runs.

Not the smile of the saint but the grimace of the tiger. Alderman had taken 4 for 68 and 5 for 62 at Trent Bridge, 3 for 59 and 5 for 131 at Headingley, and now he was back in the thick of it with 5 for 42 and 3 for 65. His leaden-footed approach is not initially a thing of beauty but there is nothing wrong with the top half of him. He is strong, well-muscled, blessed with stamina. He bowls straight, keeps the ball up, gets plenty of bounce. His pace is not exceptional, scarcely above medium-fast, but he is always doing something, and always gives the impression of performing well within himself. In addition, when not disguised by a hideous construction worker's helmet and chin guard, he has the clean-cut looks of a matinée idol, a true son, in this instance, of the surf.

LEFT Brearley's 48 in the first innings, a determined effort that lasted nearly 3 hours, was the top score of the match. Hughes, with 47, came next. Brearley, though becalmed on 13 for almost an hour, was accelerating nicely when Lillee lured him into chasing a slower, wider delivery. It was one of several such errors by England's batsmen; Boycott had gone much the same way, compulsively following Alderman's outswinger, Gower had been caught mistiming an ill-judged hook without scoring, Willey had been bowled round his legs sweeping at Bright.

A year earlier Brearley, heavily bearded and fielding in floppy sunhat, provided a fair impression of Toulouse-Lautrec. He had led Middlesex, with some assistance from the South African Van der Bijl and the West Indian Daniel, to the county championship. His own contribution had been 1335 runs at an average of 47.67, including five centuries, and five fifties.

This summer the ball had been moving even more sweetly off his bat and though Middlesex, without Van der Bijl, were not sweeping all before them in the championship they were not out of it. Once Botham's replacement became inevitable, Brearley, whatever the disadvantages, was the logical choice. Relieved of the captaincy he had been batting with renewed freedom and ease. Would he be able to continue to do so? Mostly, he was not; but the gains in other respects were incalculable. A pioneer of the headguard and of an exaggerated raising of the bat awaiting delivery, Brearley, in manner and method, has not always found favour. But he has the courage of his convictions and 1981 set the seal on his England career in no uncertain fashion.

RIGHT Hughes, sweeping at Emburey, is not out, though Taylor's anguished appeal suggests the ball might have hit the stumps.

ABOVE Lillee, never reluctant for a word, addresses Taylor, following a tête-à-tête with Gooch. Botham remains an interested observer.

RIGHT Brearley lbw to Lillee for a briskly made 13, the ball keeping low. England started their second innings 69 behind – 44 of these having been extras, Willis bowling 28 no-balls, not for the first time in these Tests – but by close of play, on a soft, cloudless evening, had reduced the deficit to 20. Lillee's delight, so acrobatically expressed, seems excessive for one of his mature years, but perhaps he was limbering up for a night out.

Suspicion of the pitch, without much evidence, resulted in further snail-like progress by England. Gower pottered uncharacteristically for 70 minutes before becoming the first of Bright's five victims. Out to a foolish stroke in the first innings, Gower never left any real mark on the series and, like Gooch, was left out at the Oval.

Bright wheeled away over the wicket, bowling sixteen overs, ten of them maidens, for 13. By lunch Boycott had reached 28 in 45 overs, allowing Bright a dominance that infected Gooch, too.

Whatever England hoped to achieve by mere occupation of the crease was not forthcoming, for Bright proceeded to remove Boycott, Gooch, and Willey in quick succession, and then bowled Gatting round his legs as he attempted a sweep.

Boycott, his rigidity of stroke exaggerated by his encased left arm, is beaten by Bright's flight and spin. Marsh loses his cap but not the ball. Sir Leonard Hutton, writing next day in *The Observer*, remarked witheringly that he would have felt 'insulted' by the imposition of such close fielders as Bright used for Boycott. What became plain was that Boycott's tactics might have been all very well if Gooch or Gower had got going at the other end, but in the event they simply turned mouldy alongside him. Boycott, one is told, can only play in his own particular way, though the evidence is all to the contrary.

LEFT No novelty about this dismissal; Botham caught Marsh bowled Lillee. If anyone could have put Bright into perspective it would have been Botham, but unfortunately Lillee removed him before he had the chance. Botham's innings lasted only 11 balls. Possibly he was suffering from Headingley-lag; alternatively, he was simply speeding up things for his second innings bowl. Old, in fact, did the job for him, making 23 in 24 balls, mostly off Bright.

ABOVE Emburey, not usually a stylish performer, here gets it all right. With the match fast disappearing from England's reach Emburey swept and drove his way to 37 not out, using his feet splendidly to Bright. Wood is the man in the flowerpot hat, thankfully too square to be in any danger. England's ninth wicket raised 50 in 73 minutes, making the final target for Australia 150.

Two balls that changed the course of the match. When Emburey bowled the first of them Australia were 87 for 3, only 63 runs from victory with Border and Yallop ensconced.

Yallop went to play Emburey to leg, the ball spun off bat and pad, and Botham, close in at silly mid-off, took the catch. Some 20 minutes and 18 runs later Border, surprised by a ball that stood up sharply and turned, could only fend it off to Gatting at short leg. Border had batted 213 minutes for his 40, as against Boycott's 190 minutes for 29.

Whereas in the facing picture the fielders feel the need to appeal and the bowler has embarked on gentle callisthenics, here they are merely holding their breath and praying Gatting does not drop it.

The door ajar, Brearley recalls Botham. Australia need 45 to win, with 5 wickets in hand. Marsh, believing they can be got in boundaries, promptly strikes one and then is bowled going for another. Bright, *opposite*, is lbw to the next ball, beaten by pace and movement off the pitch. Six runs later Lillee, *overleaf*, steers Botham to Taylor, and Taylor, diving almost too quickly, nearly drops it: Kent, already batting for over an hour, loses his head and hits all round a ball well up to him.

ABOVE Alderman is no batsman and the chances of his stumps remaining undisturbed for long were nil. The third ball did him. I might have guessed it, his attitude seems to suggest.

Some headguards are more unsightly than others, but Alderman's takes the biscuit. Or rather it gives him the appearance of a Japanese masked against infection in a Tokyo winter.

RIGHT Botham, in prizefighter attitude, after removing Kent, Australia's last hope. The shortness of the arms are offset by their thickness and strength, by the powerfulness of the torso. Kent had batted engagingly in the first innings for 46, and for almost three hours in the match.

LEFT Last day crowds at Test
Matches in England tend to come
in for a snooze as much as for
anything else. This time they had
the rare luxury of being able to
bask in the sun and in the
reflected glory of an incredible
English victory. This kind of
demonstration is usually reserved
for Royalty or for jeering at
politicians.

ABOVE Botham seems thirsty, but
he can hardly have worked up a
sweat. After all, he had taken his
five wickets in only 28 balls.
Botham's figures were 14–9–11–5.
It really seemed too easy to be
true, or to make any sense. The
whole match did not make much
sense either, except as an
example of batsmen digging their
own graves and of Brearley's cool
in a crisis.

FIFTH TEST

OLD TRAFFORD (13–18 August)

Suddenly it was summer. The blue swept across the skies of England and for a month magically stayed there. Only Old Trafford, on the first three days of the Fifth Test, seemed immune, but even there the weather relented, moving over the weekend from Lancastrian subfusc to antipodean heat and glare. England and Australia managed 231 and 130 respectively in the former conditions, 404 and 402 in the latter. A match that began with dour, strokeless struggle and inept batting by both sides blossomed. Botham once again was the agent of change. Coming in at 104 for 5, when England had watched their 101 first innings advantage melt horribly away, Botham played another innings of legendary quality. His hundred took him 86 balls, one fewer than at Headingley, and it contained six sixes and thirteen fours, the greater part of them off the new ball.

When Botham was out, England seemed saved from defeat, almost certain of victory. Knott and Emburey indulged themselves to the extent of fifties apiece and Australia were set 506 to win, with a day and two-thirds to survive.

But, strangely enough, there were moments when they looked as if they might not merely survive but actually win. Having lost 2 wickets for 24 they were, shortly before the close of play on Sunday, 198 for 3, with Yallop and Hughes almost lethargically taking the England bowling to the cleaners.

They were both out before the end, Hughes for 43, Yallop for a mellow and faultless 114.

That might have appeared to be the end of it, but it was far from it. Marsh and Border, the latter with a broken finger on his left hand, added 90 for the sixth wicket, and then Border again and Lillee 51 for the eighth. During both these partnerships the bowlers received such a drubbing that Brearley had been reduced to reluctantly defensive field settings.

Then, just before tea, Lillee flashed at Allott and Botham at second slip, leaping high and wide to his right, plucked the ball back as it seemed to fly past him.

Alderman was quickly disposed of, but Border, his hand sprayed with pain-killer, shielded Whitney from the bowling skilful enough to take Australia past the four hundred. Border, having battled through to make the slowest hundred ever made for Australia, was left 123 not out.

ENGLAND: First Innings

G. Boycott, c Marsh, b Alderman.......... 10
G. A. Gooch, lbw, b Lillee.............. 10
C. J. Tavaré, c Alderman, b Whitney........ 69
D. I. Gower, c Yallop, b Whitney........ 23
J. M. Brearley, lbw, b Alderman........... 2
M. W. Gatting, c Border, b Lillee........ 32
I. T. Botham, c Bright, b Lillee........ 0
A. P. E. Knott, c Border, b Alderman....... 13
J. E. Emburey, c Border, b Alderman...... 1
P. J. W. Allott, not out............ 52
R. G. D. Willis, c Hughes, b Lillee....... 11
Extras (lb 6, w 2)................. 8

TOTAL.....................231

Fall of Wickets: 1–19, 2–25, 3–57, 4–62, 5–109, 6–109, 7–131, 8–132, 9–175, 10–231.

Bowling: Lillee, 24.1–8–55–4; Alderman, 29–5–88–4; Whitney, 17–3–50–2; Bright, 16–6–30–0.

AUSTRALIA: First Innings

G. M. Wood, lbw, b Allott.............. 19
J. Dyson, c Botham, b Willis............. 0
K. J. Hughes, lbw, b Willis............. 4
G. N. Yallop, c Botham, b Willis......... 0
M. F. Kent, c Knott, b Emburey......... 52
A. R. Border, c Gower, b Botham........ 11
R. W. Marsh, c Botham, b Willis........ 1
R. J. Bright, c Knott, b Botham........ 22
D. K. Lillee, c Gooch, b Botham........ 13
M. J. Whitney, c Botham, b Allott......... 0
T. M. Alderman, not out.............. 2
Extras (nb 6)..................... 6

TOTAL.....................130

Fall of Wickets: 1–20, 2–24, 3–24, 4–24, 5–58, 6–59, 7–104, 8–125, 9–126, 10–130.

Bowling: Willis, 14–0–63–4; Allott, 6–1–17–2; Botham, 6.2–1–28–3; Emburey, 4–0–16–1.

ENGLAND: Second Innings

G. A. Gooch, b Alderman................. 5
G. Boycott, lbw, b Alderman............. 37
C. J. Tavaré, c Kent, b Alderman........ 78
D. I. Gower, c Bright, b Lillee........ 1
M. W. Gatting, lbw, b Alderman........ 11
J. M. Brearley, c Marsh, b Alderman...... 3
I. T. Botham, c Marsh, b Whitney........118
A. P. E. Knott, c Dyson, b Lillee....... 59
J. E. Emburey, c Kent, b Whitney........ 57
P. J. W. Allott, c Hughes, b Bright....... 14
R. G. D. Willis, not out.......... 5
Extras (b 1, lb 12, nb 3)............. 16

TOTAL.....................404

Fall of Wickets: 1–7, 2–79, 3–80, 4–98, 5–104, 6–253, 7–282, 8–356, 9–396, 10–404.

Bowling: Lillee, 46–13–137–2; Alderman, 52–19–109–5; Whitney, 27–6–74–2; Bright, 26.4–11–68–1.

AUSTRALIA: Second Innings

G. M. Wood, c Knott, b Allott............. 6
J. Dyson, run out................... 5
K. J. Hughes, lbw, b Botham........... 43
G. N. Yallop, b Emburey................114
A. R. Border, not out.................123
M. F. Kent, c Brearley, b Emburey........ 2
R. W. Marsh, c Knott, b Willis........ 47
R. J. Bright, c Knott, b Willis........ 5
D. K. Lillee, c Botham, b Allott........ 28
T. M. Alderman, lbw, b Botham........ 0
M. J. Whitney, c Gatting, b Willis........ 0
Extras (lb 9, w 2, nb 18)............. 29

TOTAL.....................402

Fall of Wickets: 1–7, 2–24, 3–119, 4–198, 5–206, 6–296, 7–322, 8–373, 9–378, 10–402.

Bowling: Willis, 30.5–2–96–3; Allott, 17–3–71–2; Botham, 36–16–86–2; Emburey, 49–9–107–2; Gatting, 3–1–13–0.

Umpires: D. J. Constant and K. E. Palmer.

England won by 103 runs.

Boycott, getting an inside edge to Alderman and being caught via his thigh by Marsh.

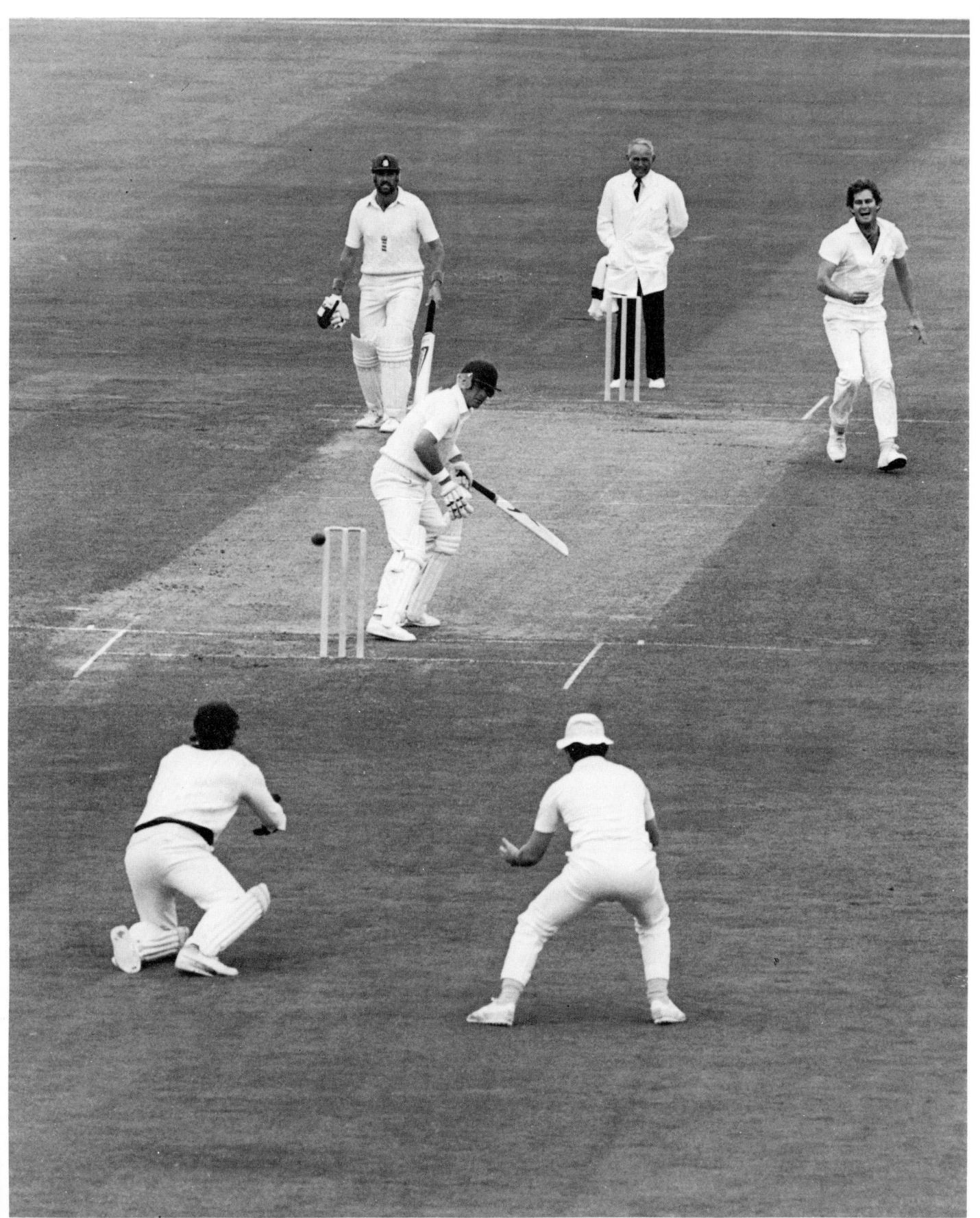

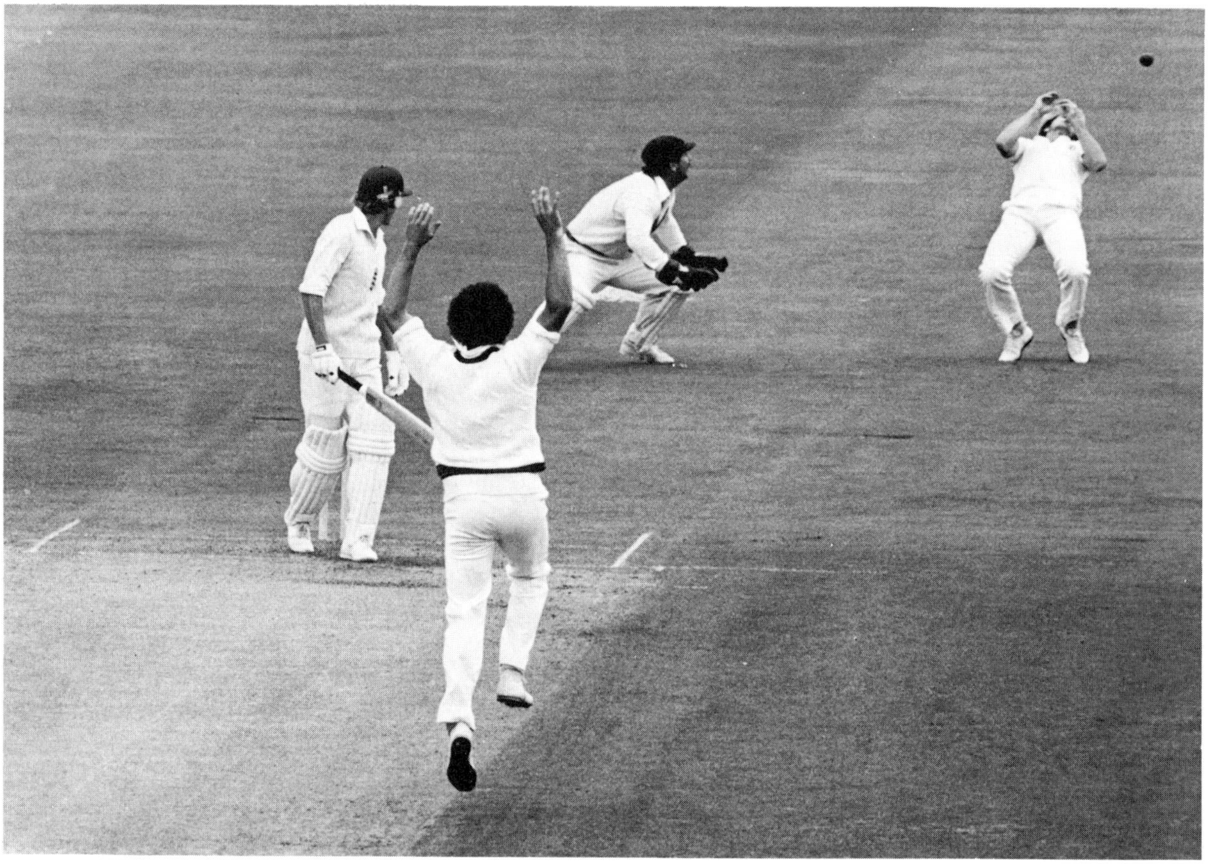

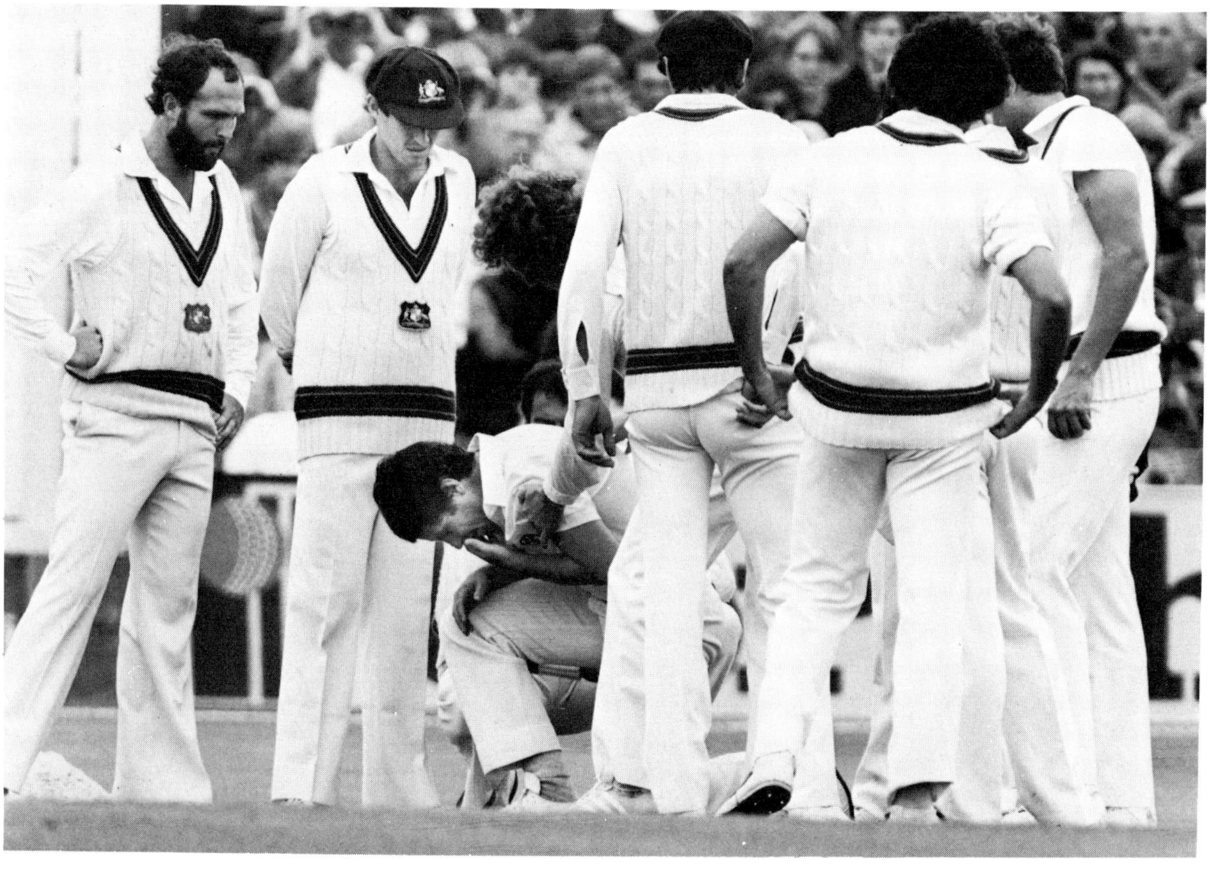

Cricket is a dangerous game, wherever you are. Wood, *top left*, fails to get his hands to the ball in time and is struck on the jaw. Gower is the lucky batsman, though he took precious little benefit from it. The Afro-hairstyled head in the foreground belongs to the bowler, Whitney, whistled out of obscurity to play his first Test match. *Bottom left*, Wood counts his teeth while his team mates commiserate. *Above*, and *right*, Border catches Emburey, but though he clings on, the ball has come awkwardly, fracturing the third finger of his left hand. It did not stop him batting for nearly 7 hours and scoring 123 not out four days later.

ABOVE The legendary hero and the aspiring acolyte. Injuries to Hogg and Lawson had caused Whitney to be hauled out of League cricket at the last minute. Bowling left-arm over the wicket at fast medium he took the wickets of Gower and Tavaré for 31 on his first day. Later he had the horrible experience of missing Botham off a swirlier skier at deep mid off during his great innings. It was a catch anyone could be forgiven for misjudging. Here Lillee seems to have some advice for him.

LEFT A moment of reflection, or homesickness. Lillee, his proper convalescence from pneumonia devoted instead to preparing himself for fast bowling, shows signs of strain. In this match Lillee, like the rest of them, took a hammering from Botham. He also took his 279th Test wicket, equalling Underwood, when Dyson took a running catch in a million on the third man boundary. Lillee, with 7 for 89 at the Oval, was soon well ahead, proving that art and intelligence, more than sheer strength and speed, keep ageing fast bowlers going. It was true of Lindwall and Trueman, once bowlers of great pace and with classical actions, and it is true now of Lillee.

The Cheshire-born Allott, given his chance on his home ground through the usual injuries to Old and Hendrick, seized it, not least as a batsman. He went in at 132 for 8 in England's first innings and was left 52 not out, spraying the ball all over the field, sometimes to the most unlikely areas. 30 was his previous best score, and 8 his batting average. He made 14 in his second innings, and took two wickets in each innings, which is what he was picked for.

Allott took only 23 wickets for Lancashire in 1980, his third season with the county. By the time of Old Trafford, however, his fast-medium seam bowling, delivered from a height of 6 foot 4 inches, had made him the leading wicket-taker in the country. Allott is 25 and wears glasses. Alderman, as usual, looks deceptively amused, though with 4 wickets to date he has good reason to be.

Decor by Cornhill, choreography and dancing by Lillee and Willis. Willis has taken a tumble trying out a new step against a Lillee beamer, but Lillee's line and gestures would get a nod from Nureyev.

Fast bowlers are rarely the bravest when on the receiving end, so usually they treat one another with exaggerated caution or try to keep out of each other's way.

Antics like these tend to lead to retribution.

Lillee's batmaker should be
pleased at the clarity of his
markings, good for trade, surely.
Lillee, when he put his mind
to it, played several useful
innings, averaging 21.85 in the
series.

LEFT It took England only 30.2 overs to bowl Australia out in their first innings for 130, a scoring rate of more than four an over, bizarre in the circumstances.

After Allott and Willis had put on 56 for the last wicket, Wood set Australia going by hooking Willis for two fours and a six in four balls. In his third over Willis took three wickets – Dyson and

Yallop both neatly picked up by Botham at slip, Hughes, as here, lbw to one that came back at him. Wood was lbw to the first ball of Allott's next over. Australia, before even the places for lunch could be laid, had slumped from 20 for 0 to 24 for 4.

ABOVE That Australia eventually reached 130, after being 59 for 6, was due largely to Kent. An upright, good-looking player Kent hit seven boundaries in his 52, the same score as Allott, though rather more of his strokes went where he intended them to. Here he hooks Willis, who has ten studs in his right shoe, and it is plain he has kept the ball down.

England, as once they used to under Brearley, caught all – or nearly all – of their catches. The difference was immense. Here Botham at third slip dives to catch Yallop, out second ball and Willis's third victim of the over. Gower was to take a fabulous catch at fourth slip before the morning was out, removing Border. Botham held a third slip catch to dispose of Marsh, also off Willis, in the second over of the afternoon.

LEFT Quicks for Ford maybe, but the slows for Tavaré, who spent four hours over 50 on the first day and got the bird. Of the 149 Botham and Tavaré put on in the second innings Tavaré's share was 28. He batted twelve hours altogether for 144.

Without Tavaré's patience and solid defensive technique, however, England might never have reached a position from which they could win. Yet there is something depressingly inert about his presence at the wicket, his limp forward stroke, often to half-volleys, dropping down on the ball with the balefulness of a tax inspector spotting a false claim. His moustache, too, drooped on a pallid countenance, seems without energy.

Looks are often deceptive, and it is too early to say whether Tavaré, as languid in manner as an 18th-century Indian Army subaltern, can shrug off his diffidence. He can bat dashingly for Kent on occasion. He has all the strokes. He takes thrilling catches at slip with the unobtrusiveness of a pick-pocket.

Mr Griffiths, apparently a peripatetic fan of Boycott, is perhaps a fan of Tavaré too. Inaction during their long partnership gave him plenty of time, as here, to do his own thing.

RIGHT Brearley, awaiting a turn at the nets on the Saturday morning. England are 171 ahead, with 9 wickets in hand. No wonder he looks happy.

ABOVE Tavaré, though he looks down mostly, must have got to know Old Trafford's advertisements by heart. He had twelve hours looking at them, not to count fielding time. His batting in this match was austerity itself; few balls got past him, he made few strokes worth mentioning. His two innings demonstrated the kind of instinct for survival torpedoed sailors display in a life-boat.

RIGHT It's going up and up and Whitney, turning round to hare after it, gets there but can't hold it. Buzby's admonishment has done the trick and *everyone* is happy, except the Australians. Botham never expected Whitney to make it and took two comfortable runs. Whitney can reflect that he showed the good sense not to interrupt a breathtaking innings.

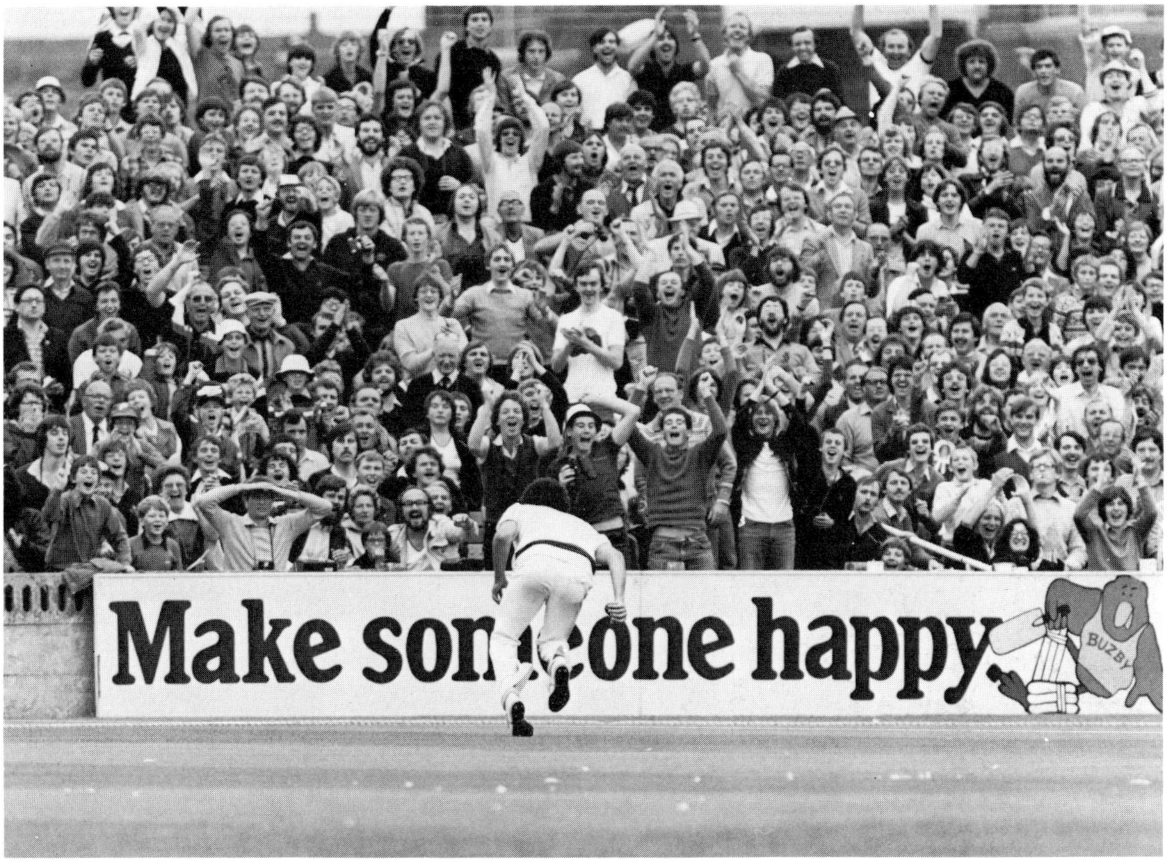
Make so
one happy
BUZBY

ber
AKEDS
rnite
Make

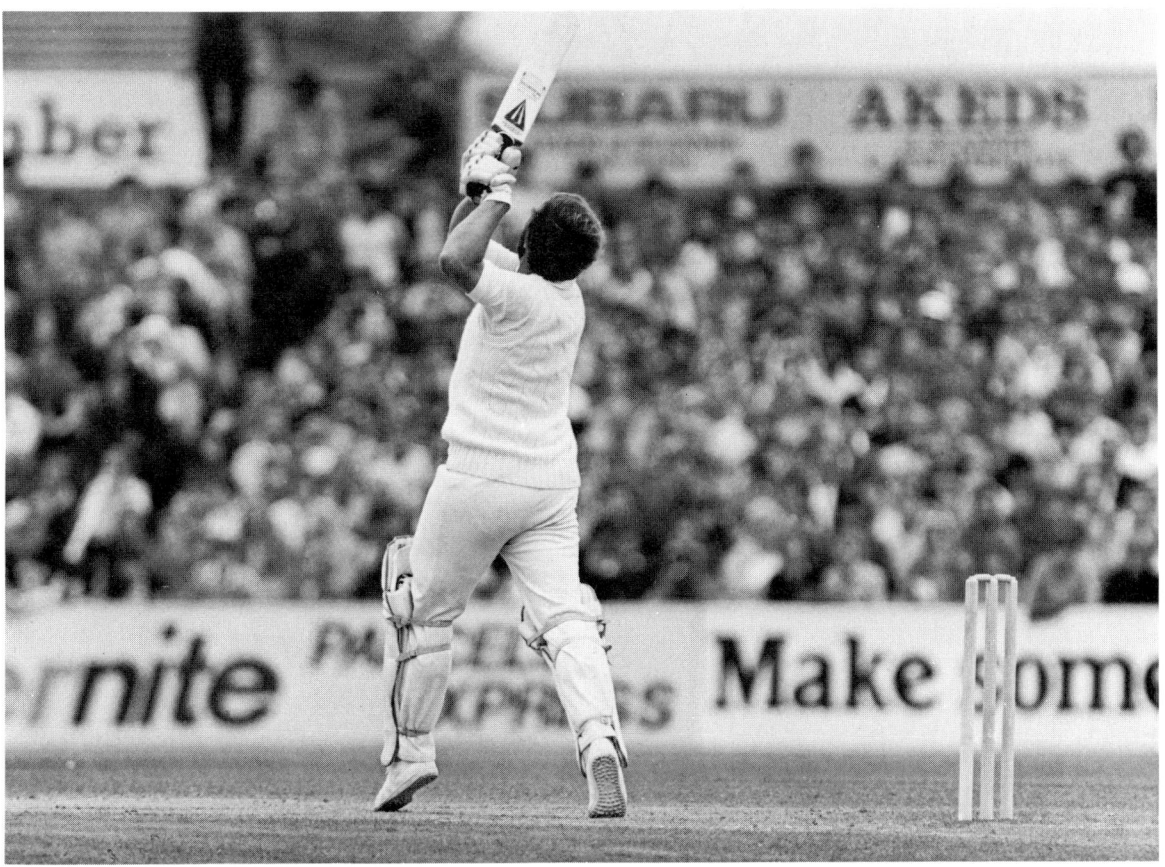

ABOVE Botham slashing, cutting, glancing, hooking. He took his time, unnervingly quiet at first, then, when the new ball was taken, cut loose. Off Alderman he took 7, 6 and 10 in successive overs; off Lillee 19, 5, 6 and 13; off Bright 8 and 7; off Whitney 1 and 8. In 53 deliveries from the old ball Botham scored 28, having made only 5 off the first 32. When he was out 13 overs later Botham had taken 90 off 49 deliveries with the new ball. He had hooked both Lillee and Alderman for six, Lillee twice dangerously late off his temple, and having swept Bright for six to reach his hundred he immediately drove him over the sightscreen for another. 'I refuse to believe,' John Woodcock wrote in *The Times*, 'that a cricket ball has ever been hit with greater power or rarer splendour.'

RIGHT The power and the glory: Lillee driven back over his head, the bat following through the line of the ball, unwaveringly.

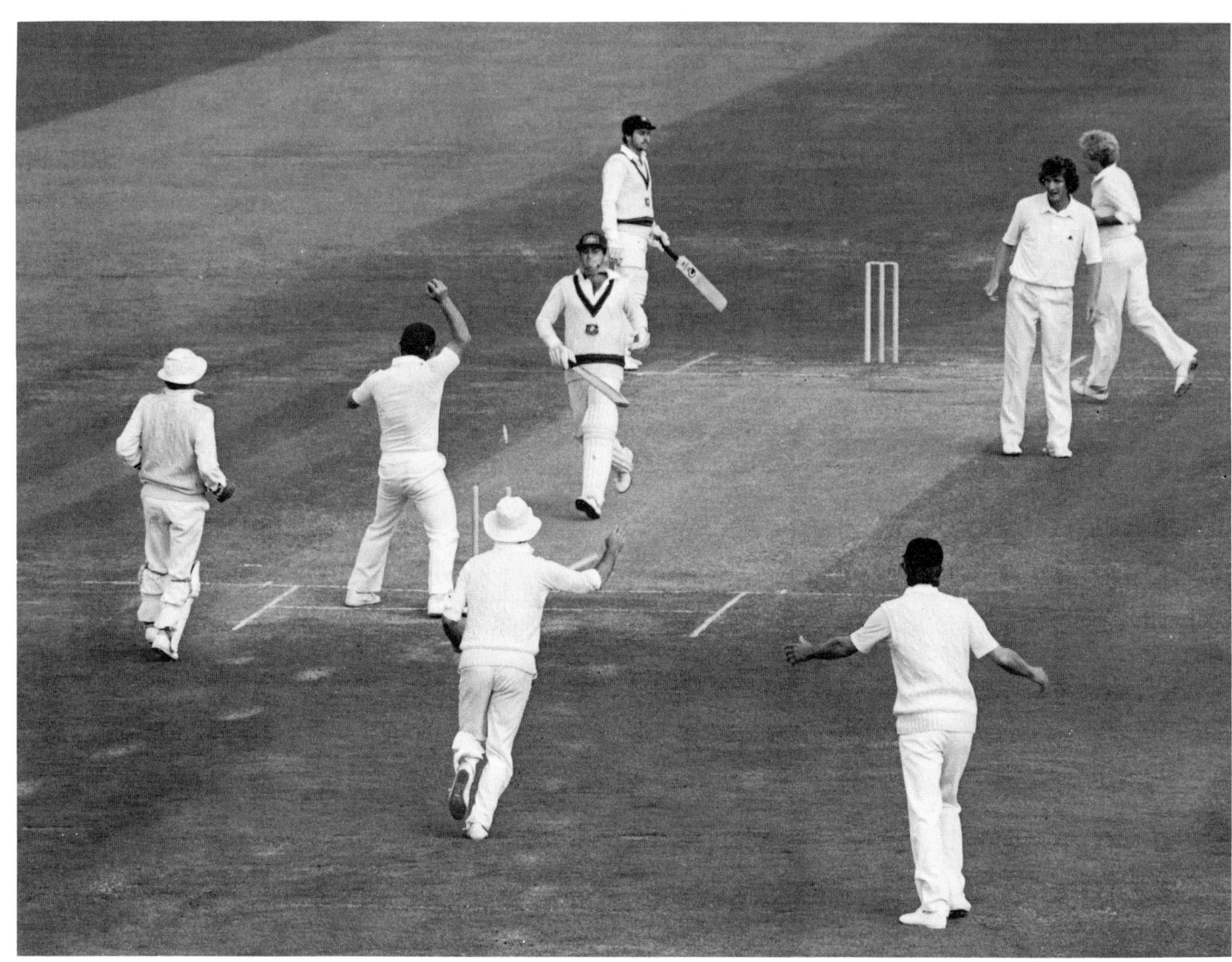

ABOVE Wood claims another victim: not a mass-murderer, but simply one of the most lethal batting partners since Compton. Dyson had played Willis to cover in the third over and called for a run. Half-way through it Wood turned tail; with Gower racing in and throwing to the batsman's end Dyson had no chance of recovery. To add insult to injury Dyson, maiden century-maker at Headingley, was dropped to make room at the Oval for Wellham, who, too, made a hundred, in his first Test.

RIGHT Yallop's shuffle to the wicket, like an arthritic old lady in slippers, belies a fine athlete. Sometimes he seemed apprehensive of short, fast bowling – who would not be? – but at his best, as in this innings, he gives off the golden aroma of good hock. Everything seems mellifluous and flowing, effortless in its stroking. He had made 114 in the most fluent manner possible against Willis, Allott and Botham when Emburey beat him in the flight and bowled him. In days not long past – during the 1978/79 fairground frenzy of Packer – he was Australia's captain. His team then was no match for Brearley's.

Marsh caught at the wicket in Willis's second over with the second new ball for 47. Marsh once made 91 against England at Old Trafford, in 1972, and he looked in the mood to make as many again. An ugly customer to bowl to, he can thump the ball with the best of them. It's always

good to see the back of him – as England demonstrate here – but it's also never dull when he's in.

Like Evans, he can get his head down surprisingly when necessary.

RIGHT Gatting catches Whitney off Willis and the Ashes are England's. But Australia, so apparently demoralized at the week-end, had salvaged much from defeat. To score 402 in the fourth innings after being 24 for 2, and still to lose by 103 runs, is scarcely a routine occurrence. Once again, though, it had been Botham's match: 0 and 118, 3 for 28 and 2 for 86, four catches, at least one of them a marvel.

Australia can rarely have batted more feebly than in their first innings. Yallop's and Border's hundreds in their second – different though they were in character – gleamed.

LEFT Border's long innings, the first of two centuries in successive Test innings and his seventh Test hundred, was a triumph over adversity, for he batted throughout with a fractured finger. Not surprisingly, *right*, he took his left hand off the bat when he could.

Scarcely ever did Border look remotely like getting out. On the last day, with the pitch playing perfectly, each Australian batsman in turn made England fight dearly for their wicket. Towards the end Border, with partners running out, kept the strike skilfully. After the match Hughes, in a tribute to Border, described him as 'a player fit to be ranked with the great left-handers'. Australia has had no shortage of these, Harvey and Morris in the post-war period among them.

SIXTH TEST

THE OVAL (27 August–1 September)

The final Test – in this case surely one too many – is either the decider or a faintly sentimental epitaph. With the series settled, this one was more in the nature of a hail and farewell party, a last chance for Kim Hughes's side to emphasize how little there was in it. This they certainly managed, England at the end being glad to hold out for a draw. But would we see Lillee or Marsh again, Brearley or Willis or Knott, perhaps not even Boycott in an Oval Test? The chances were remote for most of them. There was, then, an inevitable sadness, the first faint hint of autumn rusting the most golden of months. But if it was goodbye to some, it was also welcome to others; notably to Wellham, century-maker in his first Test after kept kicking his heels all summer. Alderman, the other newcomer, had already imprinted his name on the series.

England had less to show in this respect, neither Larkins nor Parker establishing themselves, and only Tavaré, of the less than old hands, promising any sort of permanence.

The mist that the England team had woken up to in St. John's Wood had not survived the journey to the Oval, but Brearley put Australia in all the same. Gooch, Gower and Allott had been jettisoned, Larkins, Parker and Hendrick coming in. For Australia, Kent replaced Dyson, opening the innings with Wood, Wellham taking his place at No. 6. Australia made 120 for the first wicket, the first century opening partnership for five years, and only the fourth for Australia at the Oval this century. At the close of play they were 251 for 4, Botham having had a hand in each wicket.

Australia were all out for 352, Botham finishing with 6 for 125. England, in reply, reached 246 for 2, then lost eight wickets for 68. Boycott finally made a century, his twenty-first Test hundred. Lillee took 7 for 89, his partnership with Alderman producing a record 81 wickets, ten more than Grimmett and O'Reilly shared in South Africa in 1935/6 and 31 more than the most Lillee ever took in partnership with Thomson.

Australia, largely due to Border and Wellham, were able to declare at 344 for 9, leaving England a day to make 383. At half-past two they were 144 for 6. Brearley, deservedly, now batted as he does for Middlesex, making his ninth Test fifty, though not, alas, his first Test hundred. Knott, in a Heath-Robinson kind of innings – all invention and idiosyncracy – was left 70 not out.

AUSTRALIA: First Innings

G. M. Wood, c Brearley, b Botham	66
M. F. Kent, c Gatting, b Botham	54
K. J. Hughes, hit wicket, b Botham	31
G. N. Yallop, c Botham, b Willis	26
A. R. Border, not out	106
D. M. Wellham, b Willis	24
R. W. Marsh, c Botham, b Willis	12
R. J. Bright, c Brearley, b Botham	3
D. K. Lillee, b Willis	11
T. M. Alderman, b Botham	0
M. J. Whitney, b Botham	4
Extras (b 4, lb 6, w 1, nb 4)	15
TOTAL	352

Fall of Wickets: 1–120, 2–125, 3–169, 4–199, 5–260, 6–280, 7–303, 8–319, 9–320, 10–352.

Bowling: Willis, 31–6–91–4; Hendrick, 31–8–63–0; Botham, 47–13–125–6; Emburey, 23–2–58–0.

ENGLAND: First Innings

G. Boycott, c Yallop, b Lillee	137
W. Larkins, c Alderman, b Lillee	34
C. J. Tavaré, c Marsh, b Lillee	24
M. W. Gatting, b Lillee	53
J. M. Brearley, c Bright, b Alderman	0
P. W. G. Parker, c Kent, b Alderman	0
I. T. Botham, c Yallop, b Lillee	3
A. P. E. Knott, b Lillee	36
J. E. Emburey, lbw, b Lillee	0
R. G. D. Willis, b Alderman	3
M. Hendrick, not out	0
Extras (nb 12, lb 9, w 3)	24
TOTAL	314

Fall of Wickets: 1–61, 2–131, 3–246, 4–248, 5–248, 6–256, 7–293, 8–293, 9–302, 10–314.

Bowling: Lillee, 31.4–4–89–7; Alderman, 35–4–84–3; Whitney, 23–3–76–0; Bright 21–6–41–0.

AUSTRALIA: Second Innings

G. M. Wood, c Knott, b Hendrick	21
M. F. Kent, c Brearley, b Botham	7
K. J. Hughes, lbw, b Hendrick	6
G. N. Yallop, b Hendrick	35
A. R. Border, c Tavaré, b Emburey	84
D. M. Wellham, lbw, b Botham	103
R. W. Marsh, c Gatting, b Botham	52
R. J. Bright, b Botham	11
D. K. Lillee, not out	8
M. J. Whitney, c Botham, b Hendrick	0
Extras (b 1, lb 8, w 1, nb 7)	17
TOTAL (9 wkts dec)	344

T. M. Alderman did not bat.

Fall of Wickets: 1–26, 2–36, 3–41, 4–104, 5–205, 6–291, 7–332, 8–343, 9–344.

Bowling: Willis, 10–0–41–0; Botham, 42–9–128–4; Hendrick, 29.2–6–82–4; Emburey, 23–3–76–1.

ENGLAND: Second Innings

G. Boycott, lbw, b Lillee	0
W. Larkins, c Alderman, b Lillee	24
C. J. Tavaré, c Kent, b Whitney	8
M. W. Gatting, c Kent, b Lillee	56
P. W. G. Parker, c Kent, b Alderman	13
J. M. Brearley, c Marsh, b Lillee	51
I. T. Botham, lbw, b Alderman	16
A. P. E. Knott, not out	70
J. E. Emburey, not out	5
Extras (b 2, lb 5, w 2, nb 9)	18
TOTAL (7 wkts)	261

R. G. D. Willis and M. Hendrick did not bat.

Fall of Wickets: 1–0, 2–18, 3–88, 4–101, 5–127, 6–144, 7–237.

Bowling: Lillee, 30–10–70–4; Alderman, 19–6–60–2; Whitney, 11–4–46–1; Bright, 27–12–50–0; Yallop, 8–2–17–0.

Umpires: H. D. Bird and B. J. Meyer.

Match drawn.

Wood mishooks Willis, but safely between fielders.

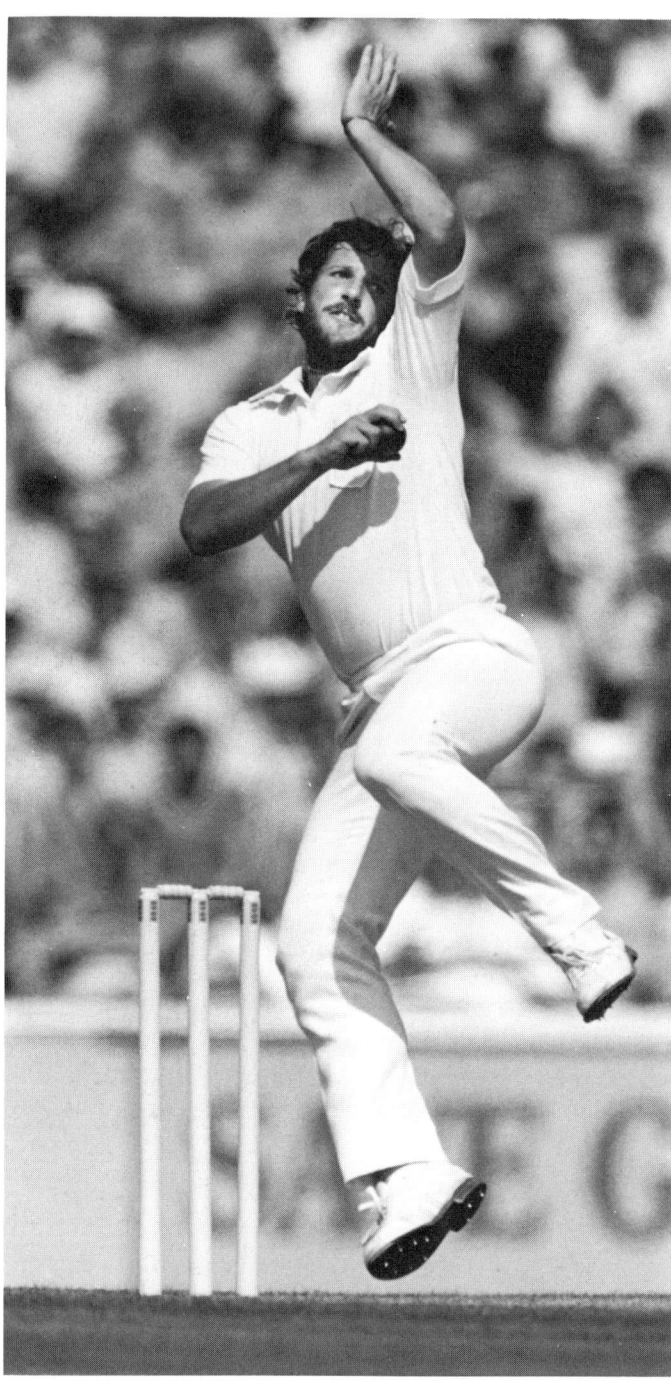

BELOW & RIGHT Hughes, hooking at Botham, dislodges a bail. Only the Australian captain, in this unluckiest of series, could have found such a way to get out.

ABOVE Botham in full sail, even to the bellying shirt. Had it not been for his three wickets and rocketing slip catch Brearley's decision to put Australia in might have made him look silly. Botham had twinges of back trouble after this match but from Headingley on he ran in with the fervour of old.

Border hooking during his second successive Test century, and, *above*, swaying from a bouncer with a boxer's practice. As at Old Trafford Border batted without chance. His technique, allowing few hostages to fortune, enlists respect rather than devotion. This was not the series – or no Australian save Yallop, once, made it appear so – for charming the bowling into surrender; in the circumstances Border's boulder-like presence was the bulwark on which England's attack repeatedly foundered.

LEFT A sight for sore eyes, or a fast bowler's revenge. Willis, having aimed more at Wellham's head than his stumps, follows up with almost a yorker. Few fast bowlers have ever been more introspective than Willis, so absorbed in their task that they scarcely take in their surroundings. Wellham had a more eloquent reply in his second innings.

BELOW Not above pocketing other men's trifles Botham catches Marsh after a ricochet off Tavaré. The bowler was Willis, though Hendrick's crucified anguish might suggest otherwise.

Boycott puts Bright away to reach his hundred and confirm his passage to India. Only in the later stages of this one innings, though, did Boycott come anywhere near to dominance. Bright looks weary, but Marsh has moved as far over to leg as any wicket-keeper could prudently go.

ABOVE Knott was brought in as
much to take Underwood as for
his batting, hitherto this summer
of negligible significance.
Underwood never played, but
Knott, magically surmounting
the gap of years, performed in the
old manner. His scores were 13,
59, 36, 70 not out, and he headed
England's averages. Here Lillee
is bowling him.

LEFT Not two Sumo wrestlers,
but Lillee embracing Yallop for
having wonderfully caught
Boycott off his bowling. At gully,
Yallop has few equals.

ABOVE Willis fails to hold
Wellham, then 18, and give
Botham what would have been
his 200th Test wicket. Wellham
was dropped again when 99, a
much simpler catch, by Boycott
at mid-off.

RIGHT Tavaré leaps, but it is no
catch. Tavaré later caught
Border off Emburey at slip for 84,
sixteen runs short of his third
hundred in a row, his second in
the match.

Marsh's last stroke of the series – perhaps his last in a Test in England – gives Botham his 200th Test wicket. From an inauspicious beginning Marsh, for all his apparent bulk, developed into the safest and most agile of wicket-keepers. Moreover, while he was batting no match was ever quite lost.

LEFT Wellham, having sailed sweetly up to 99, gets becalmed and befuddled. Only through Boycott's indulgence did he get to his hundred at all, the first such made in England by an Australian in his first Test match since 1893. A newcomer to glasses – he tried them for the first time in Sri Lanka on his way over – Wellham batted for four and a half hours. Shortest of the Australians, he gets his nose well over the line, stroking the ball through the covers off the back foot with the sweetest of timing. Only 22, he looks set for great things.

RIGHT Boycott lbw for nought and Lillee has the last laugh. It is the first over of the last day and the ball has cut back off a length. How many overs down the years, one wonders, has Lillee bowled to Boycott? Fitting perhaps that Boycott should have gone out with a hundred and a duck and that Lillee should have got him each time.

Brearley comes into his own and bows out with a fifty. Hughes seems to have spotted a snake or a Sydney cricket writer.

When Marsh caught Brearley off Lillee there were little above ten overs left. Brearley, finding some delicacy of touch and smoothing the length ball through the covers, had added 93 with Knott. He will remember his swan-song.

ABOVE Knott, looking like Salvador Dali, sweeps Bright to the boundary, a stroke to dissolve a decade. Knott, more than anyone, brought the old days back, when the word Packer was still associated with warehouses and cricketers bought their own cars.

RIGHT Last rites and fond farewells. Soon the Australians would be winging their way home, readying for Pakistan and West Indies. In November England flew off to India. The merry-go-round scarcely pauses.

It had been a sensational series, a heady, revitalizing summer for England. A triumphant return for Brearley; a legendary re-birth for Botham; a wonder for Willis.

The Australians were no slouches, except at the crisis. Two of the three Tests they lost they should have won easily; the one they had no chance in they came nearest to winning. Lillee remained a great bowler, Alderman took giant strides towards becoming one. Border scored well over a hundred runs more than any other batsman on either side.

It was anything but one-sided.

Photo: William Eagar

LEFT Now for my next trick something a little more difficult: Ian Botham at Bristol, learning to fly.

RIGHT Some strokes are easier than others; at this game your pads don't get in the way, either. Kim Hughes at Moor Park.

BELOW More comfortable than facing Lillee and Co., though those spiky figures at first slip and short leg seem unpleasantly close. Mike Brearley at Close of Play.

Photo: Jan Traylen